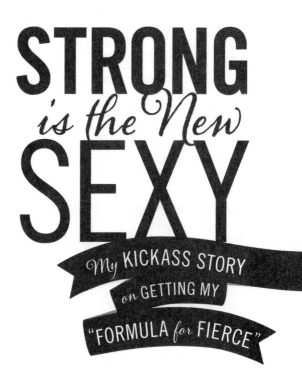

STRONG
is the New
SEXY

My KICKASS STORY on GETTING MY "FORMULA for FIERCE"

By NICOLE "**SNOOKI**" POLIZZI

RUNNING PRESS
PHILADELPHIA · LONDON

Books published by Running Press are available at special discounts for
bulk purchases in the United States by corporations, institutions, and other
organizations. For more information, please contact the Special Markets
Department at the Perseus Books Group, 2300 Chestnut Street, Suite 200,
Philadelphia, PA 19103, or call (800) 810-4145, ext. 5000, or e-mail
special.markets@perseusbooks.com.

ISBN 978-0-7624-5871-4
Library of Congress Control Number: 2015945701

E-book ISBN 978-0-7624-5876-9

9 8 7 6 5 4 3 2 1
Digit on the right indicates the number of this printing

Cover and Interior design by Sarah Pierson
Edited by Jennifer Kasius
Typography: Alana Pro, Chronicle Text, Reverie, and Trade Gothic

Running Press Book Publishers
2300 Chestnut Street
Philadelphia, PA 19103-4371

Visit us on the web!
www.runningpress.com

Contents

~

How to Be Weak

When I found out I was pregnant with my daughter, Giovanna, my first thought was, "Oh, shit! This girl is gonna kill me!"

I hoped she'd look like me because I was insanely cute as a baby. But my personality and manners? Not so adorable, especially as I got older. My parents still wake up in a cold, dank sweat, remembering certain moments from my teenage years. The idea of having a Mini-Me who would, as soon as she could talk, start telling me what to do and giving me shit, terrified me. After Lorenzo was born, I set out to get in shape to be strong enough to carry his stroller up and down a flight of stairs (essential, since I was living in Jionni's parents' basement). In a year, I lost forty pounds of fat and gained a shit ton of muscles. So, yeah, mission accomplished. But I knew I'd need a different kind of strength—along with a fit body—to keep my girl spawn in line.

Being pregnant with Giovanna raised my expectations about what a baller she was going to be. From the first quickening, she pummeled my uterus like a punching bag. I thought fetal Lorenzo might have a future as a professional kickboxer or extreme fighter. Giovanna was twenty times worse. She waged a full-scale attack on my ribs for months. I was worried she'd punch right through my stomach, and I'd see a tiny fist sticking out, giving me the finger, like, "Fuck you, Mommy! I'm sick of hanging around in here!"

If I was cranky and moody while carrying Lorenzo (and I sure as hell was), with Giovanna, I was President Evil. Jionni would shake his head at me and say, "You're so *nasty.*" Any cutting remark that popped into my head came straight out of my mouth. I often thought, *My baby girl is turning me into a raving bitch.* She gave me awful dreams about being abducted by aliens and ghosties— especially terrifying because I'm a total believer in paranormal phenomena. There were moments, private tortured moments, when I was convinced I was carrying a demon, like Rosemary's baby. As creepy as the nightmares were, I was also impressed. My girl put those images in my head? That must mean she had a big, weird, creepy imagination—and I liked it. Prenatal pride!

Then I gave birth and Giovanna and I met for the first time. From day one, she's been a beautiful angel—and a demanding diva.

Jionni and I had it easy with Lorenzo and we didn't even realize it. Giovanna's attitude is already off the charts. As a newborn, she howled like a banshee. Now, at four months old, she insists on everything being exactly how she likes it. In about thirteen years, full-scale war will break out between us. It's inevitable. I'm preparing mentally for it now. She's going to challenge me, push my buttons, make me cry, and freak me the fuck out every single day. I just know it.

Isn't it *awesome*?

I *want* her to give me hell. If I could wish one thing for my new daughter, it's that she be as tough as nails and strong as an ox. Being a woman in this world requires it.

Based on my own experience, I've been weak and soft, and not so happy. I've been strong and fit, and beyond happy. I've been a fit mom for two plus years and I've become a workout addict. Exercise is my fix. Being strong is my high. The gym is my shrink's office, my church, my retreat, the place where everything makes sense, and I always leave feeling awesome about myself. It's where I go to unload stress, gain energy, and blow off steam. Working out gives me a million benefits that help me in all areas of my life, and it's the only thing I do just for myself. I love how it feels when my muscles burn and I pour sweat. When I sniff my armpits after a workout, it smells disgusting, yes, but I always think, *Ahhh, the stink of accomplishment.*

My physical strength—seriously, check out my guns on Instagram—is the foundation of my emotional strength. My body gives me confidence, which enables me to try new things, reach for higher goals, and deal with haters on Twitter every day. It gives me energy to be a great mom and wife. It keeps me humble, too, and fills me with gratitude for being alive, being myself, and being a woman.

Strength, love, confidence, and gratitude are the fundamentals of joy. I can measure my joy right on the treadmill display screen. Five years ago, I could barely go a mile. Now I can run three miles in twenty-seven minutes. If I can do *that*, I can do anything. And if I can do anything, you *definitely* can.

I'm not saying fitness is the antidote to every horrible thing that can happen. I do think of it as a kind of shield, though. Like, "I got fired and my boyfriend dumped me, but I can still rock a bikini." It's the one variable you *can* control, so why not take it?

When Giovanna gets older, I'm not going to give her my whole sermon on strength. Why? If she's anything like me, she's just going to do the opposite of whatever I say. I'm going to have to use reverse psychology on her and trick her into being the super-strong teenager I hope and pray she'll turn out be. I've created a list of a lot of ways a woman can be a weak, pathetic loser—see below—and I'm going to preach each item to Giovanna so she does the opposite.

1. STARVE YOURSELF.

It breaks my heart when I see women starving themselves to be skinny. I did it once, when I had my high school anorexia episode. It only lasted a few months. I starved myself down to ninety pounds by eating just one cracker a day. The whole point of losing weight was to become a better cheerleader. Fail. I was so weak and exhausted that I could barely get through a practice. The school nurse told my parents that I was coming in to weigh myself every day, and that the number was getting dangerously low. Mom and Dad made me see a doctor. I talked to him about what I was doing, and opened up to my parents about it, too. Talking made me realize I was making less of myself, not more. I started eating again.

When high school ended and college began, I started drinking a lot and chowing down on junk food, and took on all the weight I lost, plus a lot more. Although I was consuming thousands of calories a day during the party years, I was actually starving myself of healthy food. The more crap I ate, the stupider I got, as seen on seasons one through five of *Jersey Shore*. When I stopped drinking and started eating lots of greens, whole grains, and lean meats, it was like my brain woke up from a five-year coma. My life turned around, and things clicked into place in my relationship and my career.

What goes into your body comes out in your life. If you want success, love, and the strength to cope with anything life throws at you, feed your body the healthy food it needs.

2. BE A DOORMAT.

Do you let people walk all over you? Do they take advantage of your generosity and good nature? Do they always call you first for big favors, free babysitting and dog walking? Are you the one they hit up for quick loans, and take for-freakin'-ever to pay you back? Has any friend, ever, asked you to help her move? Very crucial question: Do you say yes every freakin' time? If so, you are a doormat.

I want to draw a clear line between being a doormat and being a good friend. I'd do pretty much anything for a friend, even haul furniture and pack boxes. I helped my bestie Jenni move out of the house she was sharing with a horrible boyfriend years ago, way before she met her baby daddy, Roger. I was thrilled to help her that day, actually. It was an emergency situation. She had to get out right away. If she stayed for one more day, she would have been miserable. I was proud to be able to be there for my friend in her time of need. I know Jenni would do the same for me, at the drop of a hat. Friends help each other—no question.

Doormats, on the other hand, aren't operating on an equal, reciprocal level. It's one sided. One "friend" asks you to do things, but when you ask her, she makes excuses. I'm not saying you should test your friendships by asking people to do random, annoying chores for you, or to keep score. But I do believe you should search your feelings. Do you jump at the chance to do someone's bidding because you hope she'll like you more for it? Are you afraid that, if you don't buy her lunch or steal her a lip gloss, she'll dump you? In that case, if you were an actual doormat, it would read, "Wipe your feet on my face, I don't mind." You should mind! Along with your time and money, you're giving away your pride.

At the core of it, being a doormat or a people-pleaser is trying to be who that person wants you to be. That is not the way to live an honest life. Inner strength comes from being who you are, not twisting into someone else for someone else.

3. DON'T STAND UP FOR YOURSELF.

If you don't defend your own honor, it's a sign of weakness. Other people might stand up for you, and that's awesome. But you build up strength and pride by standing up for yourself.

I've been bullied many times in my life, by older girls in high school, haters on Twitter and even the governor of New Jersey (more on all of that later). What I've figured out is that the goal of the bully is to make himself feel better by bringing you down. The only way a bully can win is if you actually feel worse about yourself based on what they say or do. Usually, the bully has no idea who you really are. Even if they see you every day like at school or work, they're not in your head and heart. They don't know your thought and private feelings. Therefore, the insults are *always* about the person who makes them, and have nothing to do with you.

I'm not saying being bullied is easy. When a thousand people called me a fat troll whore on Twitter every day during the height of *Jersey Shore*, I had to dig deep into my core inner strength to remind myself, "I'm a good person. I love my family and friends and I'd never hurt a fly." As long as you remember the truth about your soul, you won't sink into anger, sadness or embarrassment about the ravings of douchebags. They don't know you. Only you know you. If you're still in the process of getting to know yourself, don't let the bullies fill in the blanks. Do that for yourself, by proving you're a strong, powerful person who laughs in the face of assholery.

4. FEEL JEALOUS OF OTHER WOMEN.

"There's a special place in hell for women who don't support other women," said former Secretary of State Madeline Albright. Or maybe that was Beyoncé? Doesn't matter. Who ever said it, I agree. Unless it's on the soccer (or whatever) field, girls shouldn't compete against each other. Women should empower each other. I see a lot of women on the Internet who say very nasty crap about one another. Fuck that. Build each other up, boo boos, especially if you are doing what you love and supporting yourself and your kids.

It makes me sick to see women bring each other down for no reason. Why is it so often about how we look and what we eat? I'd say there's an even darker corner of hell for women who try to tear other women down about their appearance, calling them fat, ugly hots and cows. We're not barnyard animals. We're women doing our best with what we've got. Same goes for those who criticize a woman for being too thin or too shot full of Botox. It's none of their business what Kelly Clarkson weighs or what Renée Zellweger did to her face. I get why fans track the ups and downs of celeb weight and why plastic surgery "Did She or Didn't She?" photos are on the covers of magazines. It's like the sports pages for women. Guys obsess about batting averages and completion percentages of their favorite players. Women are fascinated by the body fat percentages of celebrities. I admit I look, and then I need a sandblaster shower.

I hold a special disgust for women who criticize others for their fashion choices. Shows like *Fashion Police* really piss me off. I'm glad it got canceled. (I love some of the hosts as people; I just despise what they do.) We all feel comfortable in our own way, and as long as you think you're pretty in what you wear, that's all that matters. There are no fashion fails. Anyone can wear whatever she wants. Hey, a garbage bag with a belt can be a cheap-yet-stylish look. If you love it, you rock it, and don't care what anyone says. I've made a point of catching myself when a negative or critical thought comes up, and replacing it with a positive one. I look at a woman dressed in a weird way, and say, "Good for her! She's rocking that clown suit."

Let's try and stop judging each other. Even if you think a friend's outfit is hideous, say it in your head. To her, say, "Rock on." Woman-on-woman criticism about appearance only makes it harder for everyone who wasn't born with Kendall Jenner's body (aka, every women who ever lived except her). We're all doing the best we can with what we've got. We should all be appreciated and praised for that. Just saying.

5. SAY "FUCK IT."

Not giving a crap what anyone thinks of me has gotten me through some rough times, especially when I first announced my pregnancy with Lorenzo, and the whole world seemed to think I'd be an unfit mother. Did they really believe I'd do vodka shots with a baby on the way? Really? I was barely drinking at that point in my life. If the critics knew me at all, they wouldn't have accused me of prenatal child abuse. So I brushed it off my shoulder like lint. Being able to say, and really feel, "I don't care," is a gift. The people who mattered to me—my friends and family—were thrilled for Jionni and me about the pregnancy. They knew how excited we were and that I'd do anything to make a healthy baby. I just went on with my life, and have since proved all the doubters wrong.

But—there is a giant gap between the "I don't care" and "fuck 'em all" mind-sets. "Fuck 'em all" comes from a place of anger. Your actions will be motivated by spite, which takes you in a different direction than not letting assholes get to you. Spite can make you lose sight of what you *do* care about. When I was at my highest weight, I would talk myself out of getting in shape on the grounds that, "I don't care what people say. I think I look great, so fuck it," and then I'd eat a ton of fried pickles.

It was like I had to prove to other people that I wouldn't change myself just because they were critical about my weight. I had to peel away a few layers of emotions before I could admit to myself that I really didn't look so hot and that I needed to do something about it. Getting in shape and losing weight wasn't giving in to critics. It was taking care of myself. Now, when I look in the mirror, I can say, "I do care, and I'm fabulous."

In a nutshell: Figure out what matters to you, and care *a lot* about it. Don't give a crap about what others throw at you. Just flick off the bullshit, and get on with your life.

6. BE SUPER CAREFUL.

Eleanor Roosevelt once said, "Courage is more exhilarating than fear." Anything that gets your heart pumping and stretches your limits takes courage. And courage about trying new things definitely makes you strong and flexible. Flexible is its own kind of strength, which is why I do yoga sometimes. Not too often. I'm not a hippie like that.

Being too cautious does the opposite. It makes you weak. If I were super careful, I wouldn't have auditioned for a new MTV reality show back in 2009. If I were afraid of making a fool of myself, I wouldn't have appeared on *Dancing with the Stars*. I threw caution to the wind, and went for it. I got the MTV job, and became famous. I ballroom danced on national TV, made great friends, had a blast, and learned some new moves. Every single time I had to find courage to do something—from writing a novel to becoming a wife and mommy—it's taken me to amazing new places. You could say being reckless made my life and my career what it is today.

My attitude is, don't think so hard. Being too smart is a kind of stupid. When caution calls the shots, you miss out on the fun and rewards of taking risks. So what if you fall flat on your face sometimes? It happens. But I've learned more from my failures than my successes, and I've had plenty of both. Besides, falling on your face is freaking funny. You never laugh so hard you cry about all the times you were perfect and everything went as planned. You look back and laugh about the mistakes, the batshit crazy stuff that goes horribly wrong. Be messy and take risks. Make mistakes, learn from them, and then crush it the next time around. Don't be so afraid to fuck up that you play it safe. I think we've all figured out by now, thanks to a thousand reality competition shows, that playing it safe is like giving up.

7. HAVE ALL THE ANSWERS.

Who is the most annoying person in the room? The one who has all the answers and is always right. He (it is usually a he) has opinions on everything, corrects you, and generally thinks his poop smells like roses. The last thing any woman needs is some dude telling her the way things are. Attention mansplainers: You don't learn anything in life by listening to yourself blah, blah, blah. Being right is so boring. Interesting people are curious about what others think and feel. Even someone as self-centered as I am knows that you have to shut up and listen some of the time.

In my book (which you are reading), it's way more interesting to be clueless. If you start at zero, you have nowhere to go but up. When you start at zero, you're open to new ideas and experiences. You don't have preconceived notions about what you're capable of. If you knew everything, you'd know your limits. But if you have no friggin' idea what's going on, the sky's the limit.

I can't help thinking about my utter cluelessness as a new mom. Jionni and I asked a million questions, and learned by doing out of sheer necessity. We didn't know how to change a diaper. When you've got a newborn, you figure it out quick or you're up to your own eyeballs in shit. My parenting skills got really strong, really fast, in part because I didn't know the "right way." I just did what I had to do my way, and it turned out to be just fine. Better than fine—great. If being wrong makes you strong, I don't ever want to be right.

8. GIVE UP.

The ultimate enemy of strength is laziness. It's also one of the hardest habits to break. My lazy years started when I quit cheerleading in high school. I stopped practicing for hours a day, and replaced the exercise with partying. I went to clubs every weekend with the girls. I ate and drank and stayed out until 3:00 a.m. During the Party Era, I started to take on weight. I was heavy for me when I auditioned for *Jersey Shore,* and then put on another twenty pounds. It might not seem like a lot, but I'm only four foot nine inches. When we shorties gain two pounds, it's like ten for a regular size person. My torso is so tiny, even five pounds gets scrunched down and looks like an inner tube around my waist. I was shocked by how heavy I looked in photos, but I still didn't want to scale back on drinking. I was living it up, enjoying myself and not worrying about a thing. I tried sporadically to get back to the gym. I'd go on Monday, Tuesday, and Wednesday, but if I didn't see results right away, I'd blow it off for the rest of the week, and the next week. If you're discouraged, it's hard to get into the groove.

And then I met Jionni. He's athletic and loves to work out. I wanted to be sexy for my new man, and I started to hit the gym again. I lost weight, and looked pretty good, but it wasn't to last. My hotness had to be put on hold due to our unplanned pregnancy. For nine months, I gave myself permission not to worry about my weight. I didn't exercise, I ate like a buffalo, and gained fifty pounds. Again, a typical gain for a medium-size person. But for me, I put on half my pre-pregnancy body weight! I was a person and half. Not cool.

After Lorenzo was born, I set my mind to being the person I pictured myself to be—a superfit, superstrong MILF who could keep up with my baby, lift the car seat without breaking a sweat—and I went for it. I hit the gym as soon as the doctor said I could. I stuck with it, and really got into my workouts. Even when I was exhausted from being up all night with the baby, I worked out. I missed Lorenzo when I was at the gym, but it was good to get out of the house and take care of myself. I was a better mom for it. I started to think of my sessions with my trainer, Anthony, as mini-vacations, even though he was tough on me and really made me sweat. The weight didn't fall off. It took six months to see results, which was frustrating as you can imagine. If I didn't have motivation and the need to burn off steam, I probably would have given up after a few weeks.

Anthony explained that you gain muscle while you lose fat, so your weight stays the same even though you're working hard. So after months of hard work, I started to notice the change. I had more muscle definition, a smaller waist, toned legs, and I really felt my physical power. My body was stronger, but I'd also proven to myself that I could stick to it. Even better than muscle power is the power of determination and dedication. I'd passed through laziness, discouragement, and pain to get to the other side of feeling proud and accomplished. Fitness is so much bigger than being thin or having toned legs. It's knowing that you can set a goal and reach it—and fall in love with yourself in the process.

Anyone can transform herself into the person she always wanted to be. I hated the gym. I hated running. Now, I love doing push-ups. I drop and give myself twenty. If you have a slow start, don't get discouraged. You will get there. Work hard for goals, and trust me, you'll be amazed by what you're capable of. When you tap into that bottomless well of "hell yes," suddenly everything else in your life will seem a lot easier.

I could write an entire book about physical strength—how to get it, how awesome it feels—but, to me, strong in body gets you only halfway to she-leopard. What accounts for the other half?

Not "strong in mind," because then I'd be screwed.

It's a strong sense of self, solid relationships, a clear vision of what you want, and being grateful for all of it. When you balance emotional strength with physical power, you feel the force in your body, heart, *and* soul. You're unbeatable. I believe there's an undeniable connection between running on a treadmill and chasing away your demons. If a woman builds her muscles and her confidence, no one can take her down.

Strong Is the New Sexy tells the story of how I became a fit momster and how I learned to tap my inner strength. I'm not a trainer or a shrink, and don't claim to be an expert on fitness, nutrition, and psychology. I'm not a life coach or a professional organizer. But I am an expert on how I've transformed my body and mind-set. People call me a role model for healthy eating and fitness, as unlikely as that might seem. Let's be honest, five years ago, most of the people who saw me on TV thought I'd wind up in rehab, a psych ward, or prison. Well, I've proved all those people wrong. (Technically, I did go to jail for one night, but it was so short, I didn't even have the opportunity to go lesbo.) I have figured some things out about how to be strong. It's all in this book. I hope you get some ideas or take inspiration from my stories and advice and find your own formula for fierce.

CHAPTER ONE

Strong Love

I'm married, bitches!

Finally.

Jionni and I had a strong bond before we said "I do." We had two kids and built a house together, but nothing really seals the deal like a legal document. The knot is officially tight now. As Jionni says, "Tight as a noose." He thinks he's very funny. He's got a lot to learn.

I know people say, "I don't need a piece of paper." You might not *need* it. But I, for one, *wanted* it. The piece of paper is like a pair of fur-lined handcuffs that lock you together. According to our marriage license, verified by the state of New Jersey, Jionni is my property, and I'm his. The only way he's getting out of this marriage is if I kill him first. That's not going to happen, because I'd really miss him.

Our relationship had been through a lot of changes. We started as a casual fling. Then we were friends with benefits. Then we decided to be exclusive and called each other boyfriend and girlfriend. Next, I got pregnant with Lorenzo, and we got engaged, making us fiancés. Then we were baby daddy and baby mama. And now, we're husband and wife.

Most people do this in a different order. But we're not most people.

Did you see that movie *The Five-Year Engagement* with Emily Blunt and Jason Segel? No? Me neither. If a movie doesn't have aliens, ghosts, zombies, Vin Diesel, or Ben Affleck, I have zero interest. Anyway, the premise of this movie does ring (wedding) bells for me. It's about a couple that gets engaged, and then, for a hundred reasons, can't get around to planning a wedding. The movie came out the same year Jionni and I got engaged, and I remember thinking at the time, "No way in hell is that going to happen to us." Kewl. It totally did.

Waiting to become a wife was an endurance test, like the SATs or a marathon. I sucked at the SATs. My score was 200, the amount they give you to fill in your name. And I've never run a marathon. I made it from engagement to marriage like a boss, though. No matter how long it took, I was not going to be denied My Special Freakin' Day. Oh, it sucked having to wait. Patience is one muscle I will never stop needing to develop.

HERE'S STEPHANIE

Hey. This is Stephanie, Nicole's oldest friend. If you're a fan of hers, you probably know who I am. I've appeared on her shows a few times. To be honest, I always found it awkward to "just act like yourself" with a camera in my face and four strangers watching. Nicole knew that, and respected my reluctance to be on camera. I only agreed when she pulled out the "just do it for me" card. It's our understanding that we'd do anything for each other. For me, that means going on TV.

I remember clearly when I realized Jionni was the one for Nicole. It was around three years ago. A big group of us went to Las Vegas for New Year's Eve. Nicole and Jionni got in a fight. She was crying about it to me on the balcony of her hotel room. She said, "For the first time, I can imagine spending my life with someone."

My best friend really loves this guy, I thought, and told her, "You need to tell him that."

She ran to apologize to him about whatever set off the fight, and everything was fine again between them. I saw them later that night, and he was just so sweet. He was a great guy from day one, and he genuinely cared about her— and us. Nicole comes with a lot of old friends, and Jionni didn't shy away from us. That was a good sign. Nicole had dated some guys who were more interested in who she was as

> *Snooki. Jionni fell in love with Nicole.*
>
> *Now, they're just a great couple. They laugh at each other and at themselves and they make everyone else laugh around them. You can see the dynamic on TV when they do the reaction segments together. They're constantly joking around, teasing each other. They're always in a good mood, making everyone else smile. You can't help but have fun with them.*

Jionni and I could have had a quickie wedding after he proposed on Valentine's Day, 2012. But I was already a few months pregnant with Lorenzo, and feeling the first-trimester symptoms like a ton of bricks had landed on my uterus. Even that night, I dry heaved in the toilet and was so full of gas, I could have floated to the moon. My skin was starting to break out, and I just felt gross. The day of my wedding, I'd envisioned looking like a beautiful sexy princess in my gown, not a beached whale under a tarp. I wanted to be able to drink the champagne when people made the toasts. So we decided the wedding would have to wait until after Lorenzo was born.

When the baby arrived, we focused on taking care of him. We were living in Jionni's parents' basement at the time. The crib was on one side, and our bed on the other. If we got married then, would he carry me over the threshold of his mother's house? That did not feel right. To be a real wife, I needed a real home. So, Jionni and I started looking, and found an empty lot in a new subdivision in a town nearby. We bought it. Jionni designed our dream house, and we hired a contractor to build it.

Even when the lot was just a pile of dirt, I started fantasizing about living there. I got this picture in my head of getting ready for my wedding in the upstairs master bedroom with my mom and my bridesmaids around me. When it was time, a white limo would pick me up in the circular driveway to take me to the church. Most important, after the ceremony and reception, Jionni and I would return to our home, and start our lives in the house where we'd raise our kids, and get old and wrinkly together. Once I locked in on this vision, I was not going to get married any other way.

Welp, building our house took twice as long as we thought. In the meantime, we got pregnant again with Giovanna. Our little family spent another hot, long summer sweating balls in the basement. During that time, I kept myself busy and distracted by planning our wedding. We had a moving date (September), a due day (October), and our wedding date (November). I think three of the most stressful things you can do in life are have a baby, move, and get married. We were going to do them all, within three months. I must have been insane. Only a psycho bitch would attempt this. That's me: class A psycho bitch.

Everything fell into place, right on schedule. We moved in. Giovanna arrived almost two years to the day of Lorenzo's birth. I had a little time to get back into shape postbaby to fit into the gown I bought a year earlier. I nailed down all the wedding details— invites, flowers, music, food, photographer, videographer, venue, dresses, bachelorette party, the list goes on and on, as anyone who's thrown a wedding knows. Finally, finally, finally, just as all the pieces were in place, our wedding date arrived.

My Special Freakin' Day

Our big day was *huge*. I'd been dreaming of my wedding my whole life, and I went all out. There were so many Insta-worthy, and we snapped them all.

When all my bridesmaids and I got ready in the kitchen. The room was bursting. Jionni and I had an enormous wedding party. He had seventeen ushers, and I had seventeen bridesmaids. Who the hell were they? Does a normal person have seventeen best friends? No. It was kind of ridiculous. I asked my crew from back in the day—way back, from preschool—including Stephanie, my bestie since we were three. I asked my *Jersey Shore* roomies, Deena and Sammi, and, of course, my *Snooki & Jwoww* costar and best friend, Jenni. Plus, there was Jionni's sister, and sisters-in-law.

The numbers add up fast. The whole crew and I hung out in our bathrobes, getting our hair and makeup done, drinking mimosas, and laughing our asses off all morning. My ladies looked gorgeous in the universally flattering Gatsby-inspired dresses I picked out. They will deffo wear those dresses again.

When I first put on my gown and veil, and posed for the photographer in my bedroom, holding Giovanna. She was only a couple of months old, but she got a custom-made white gown to wear, too. It turned out to be a good thing we had our babies before we got married. Giovanna in her sweet dress and Lorenzo in his handsome suit got to be in all the pictures the day their mommy and daddy got hitched. It was such a precious moment when Lorenzo walked down the aisle with his finger knuckle-deep up his nose. My baby picks boogers like a champ. He takes after his father.

When I stood on the second-floor landing in my full wedding outfit with the veil and bouquet and shoes for the first time, with my bridesmaids waiting at the bottom of the stairs, they *awwed* and said the words I wanted to hear: "beautiful," "angel," and "princess." I picked the gown by Eve of Milady because it was so traditional and princessey, with poufy sleeves, and frilly lace. I felt like Cinderella going to the ball. No glass slippers, though. I had pearl-and-diamond embellished wedges. Comfortable, and sexy.

When I cried for the first time of many that day. Two enormous flower arrangements were delivered while I got dressed. My dad put them on a table in the front hall. My parents and bridesmaids watched as I opened up the cards to see who they were from. The cards said, "From your baby girl" and "From your baby boy." Obviously, Lorenzo and Giovanna didn't send them. Jionni did. Cue waterworks! I just lost it. We all did. My father cried so hard, he couldn't breathe.

When I walked to the vintage white limo that took me to the ceremony, three of my bridesmaids had to hold my veil so it wouldn't drag on the driveway. Dad and I rode to the church together. He said, "You're all grown-up. You're not my baby anymore. I'm very, very, very proud of you," and then started blubbering. I wanted to punch him. When he cries, I start going, and I didn't want to ruin my makeup. Don't get me wrong. I'm thrilled my parents are proud that I've grown into the woman they always told me I could be. It means so much to share this day with them and . . . oh, shit. Now I'm feeling emotional *again* as I type this.

When I arrived at church. Before, back at the house, I'd been nervous about everything, and did a shot of vodka to calm me down. It didn't exactly work, and I was still anxious as we rode to church. We arrived to find dozens of paparazzi waiting outside. Seeing all those cameras got me excited. It was like being Beyoncé for a day—way better than being Cinderella. The wedding started to feel real to me. The dream was becoming a reality.

So I went into the church, and had to wait in a room for the wedding to start. I told one of the ushers, "I'm going to poop my pants." He said, "You're wearing a dress." Very fucking funny. The music started. Our enormous wedding party filed down the aisle. And then it was my turn.

When I walked down the aisle, and kept my eyes on Jionni in his tux at the altar. The man of my dreams was smiling at me, waiting for me to join him. It was an incredible rush. I loved him ten times more than I ever thought possible at that moment. I kept thinking, *I love him and he's mine.* I also thought, *Why didn't I spit out my gum? And, Would it look bad if I let out a big fart right now?* (Nerves affect my guts like green tea. I was pinching my butt cheeks the whole walk down the aisle.) The crazy, stupid things that go through your mind when you're two seconds from getting married, I had no idea.

When I got to the altar and the priest started talking to us about what it means to get married. No other word describes the feeling of being up there, in front of all those people, than "jitters."

The planning and waiting to get to this moment made me quake. My lips were quivering. My hands were shaking. I was so terrified to mess up my part in the ceremony, my legs were trembling. I also felt shakey from having so much love for Jionni. The emotions were overwhelming. I had to leave my body, and watch myself from above. It was an out-of-body experience.

When we exchanged vows. Jionni and I promised to be there for each other, in good times and bad, to stay together until death, to raise good Catholic children. While we were saying these important vows to each other, Jionni broke eye contact for a second. I said, "Look at *me*!" When I pictured this moment, I saw us staring into each other's eyes *the whole time*. When he glanced down, I had to bring him back up. He busted my balls about it afterward, how I yelled at him in the middle of our ceremony. My first nag as a wife. (Get used to it, babe.)

When we slipped on our rings, both of which were made by B&B Jewelry in Totowa, New Jersey. Mine was a copy of the band on my engagement ring, so they'd look awesome together. Jionni's ring was a copy of Brad Pitt's wedding band. My husband is obsessed with Johnny Depp and Brad Pitt. We looked online and couldn't find a good picture of Johnny's ring, so we went with Brad's. It's two gold bands fused together with diamonds embedded on the side. I also gave him a rinky-dink cheap ass ring to wear when he'd be doing yard work or playing sports. Now, someone might say, "Why doesn't he just not wear a ring when he's shoveling snow or playing golf?" I don't care what he's doing, he could be swimming in an ocean of shit, my man will wear a damn ring 24/7 that tells the world he is mine. I wear my rings that say I'm his. It's only fair. So shut up, Jionni, and put on your ring! (See what I mean about nagging?)

When we kissed for the first time as husband and wife. Jionni came in for a peck in the lips. My mind was going a million miles a minute. I was thinking, *Holy fuck, we're married. I just swallowed my gum. I have to poop. Now what do we do?* I was so stuck in my thoughts, I wasn't aware of what was going on. The kiss came as a surprise, and it was over before I knew it happened. So I grabbed him by the neck, and brought him down to give me another one, a nice, juicy kiss, to savor the moment and seal it in my mind forever.

When we arrived at the Venetian—the catering hall in Garfield, the best in New Jersey, the number one venue for weddings on the East Coast—and saw the reception room. I flipped shit. It was exactly as I'd envisioned it. They did it up right, with the chandeliers and centerpieces, totally nailing our Gatsby theme.

Walking in there was like zooming back in time to the 1920s (although I don't think they had LED lights, a fog machine, and video monitors back then). As a bride, you plan and plan, you obsessively search Pinterest for decoration ideas, you describe what you want in a hundred meetings—and then you walk into the space you created, and it's beyond your wildest dreams. It was an exhilarating moment. You get one day in your whole life to be the star of your own fantasy. On my day, the Venetian set the scene perfectly. They gave me an official helper, an adorable young woman, to tell me where to go and what was happening. She was my little bitch for the night, and she was phenomenal. Everyone there did a great job feeding and entertaining our four hundred guests. I didn't know half of them. Jionni's parents and my family invited the second cousin from Florida that just *had* to be there, who I wouldn't know if they pissed on me. It didn't matter.

When we got a look at the cocktail-hour spread. It had *twenty* food stations—pasta, seafood, roast beef, homemade mozzarella. There was a suckling pig on a spit wearing a pair of sunglasses (not Snooki Shades, I noticed). I could have fed my family for a year at that cocktail hour. I didn't get to eat any of it, though. I was upstairs in a private area, changing into dress number two. My reception dress was fun, flirty, and sleek, by Ines Di Santo. It was my "go crazy, no nuts" look, long-sleeved, lacy, silvery dress, fitted tight to my body and thighs, and then a detachable mermaid skirt so, when dancing started, I could take it off and frolic. From behind a curtain, I peeked at our guests enjoying the cocktail hour. That was the whole point: To throw an awesome party that people loved and would remember forever.

FYI: I read reports after the wedding in the tabloid trash mags that I got my wedding for free. I *wish*. I paid for every piece of shrimp, every slab of filet mignon, and every glass of prosecco. I don't get stuff for free. With the exception of my two dresses, I wrote checks for everything. People, I'm not Kim Kardashian! If I want stuff, I have to pay for it.

When we were announced as Mr. and Mrs. LaValle, my hubbie and I stood behind a curtain at the top of a long, curved staircase. The curtain opened and our guests on the dance floor below could see us on the landing in all our glory. Eight hundred eyes locked on us—not a comfortable feeling. I was convinced I was going to slip in my six-inch glitter heels and fall down the stairs. But Jionni held my hand and kept me steady. I thought, *My man is going to keep me from falling on my face for the rest of my life.* Cue happy tears . . . again. Warning to brides: You will cry twenty times at your wedding. You will blow your nose disgustingly. Your friends will cry, and snot will flow for them, too. Your parents will blubber. The happiest day of your life will be a sobfest from beginning to end, so make sure you carry tissues and use waterproof mascara.

I took Jionni's name. I was a Polizzi for twenty-seven years. I still am professionally. But personally, my name matches my husband's. By becoming a LaValle, I wasn't betraying the Polizzi name. I'm not giving up my identity. I know a lot of women feel like taking your husband's name means you become his property, and maybe that's how it used to be in the oldie days. But I feel that taking his name means he's bringing me into his family, that I'm one of them. Our children are LaValles. We are family and we all have the same name. If I kept my maiden name, they'd all be LaValles, and I'd be the only Polizzi. I'd feel left out, like I intentionally kept myself apart. That was the opposite of what getting married meant to me. We were uniting our lives, linking ourselves together in every possible way. We share everything: our time, our dreams, our house, our kids, our money, and our name.

When we ran under the bridge. We survived the walk down the stairs, and our guests clapped and cheered. *Yay! They didn't break their necks on their wedding day!* Our bridal party stood in two rows and made a bridge with their hands for us to run under. We're so short, we barely had to duck down. I giggled the whole time. As Jionni ran, he tapped his friends in the balls. He thought that was hilarious. According to my hubbie, this is appropriate wedding behavior. What is wrong with him? I was soaking in the romance, and my husband was flicking his pals' nuts.

When Jionni and I had our first dance to Lana Del Rey's "Young and Beautiful." The fog machine was pumping. The dance floor was lit up purple. It looked and felt like we were dancing on a magical cloud. I know that sounds corny, but when you're a new bride, you pile on the cheese, and it's awesome. We did the steps we rehearsed. Spin out, spin in, dip, stare into each other's eyes, smile blissfully, be super romantic. We practiced a hundred times at home, but until we did the dance at our actual wedding, I didn't feel the love as powerfully. When we were alone out there, on the cloud, with the lights and the music and the loving energy washing over us from our guests, I just kept thinking, *I love you, you're the one. I love you, you're the one.* It was a glorious moment.

When Dad and I had our father-daughter dance. Dad and I started dancing, and it was sweet. But then he told me to look at the video screen that appeared suddenly on the wall. A video montage of me through the years started playing, including photos of my grandparents who had died, and my uncle who had passed. Eye faucets open *again,* especially from Dad. It only confirmed in my mind the bonds I have with the Polizzis, my first family. That will never change, no matter what my last name is.

When Jionni and I cut the cake. I don't remember eating anything at the wedding. I was too busy dancing and making the rounds, meeting a hundred cousins. I'd taken off the mermaid part of the dress by then, and had to change my shoes, too, because I broke a heel dancing so hard. The whole night went by in a blur. It seemed like it was just starting and then we were called to cut the five-tiered, gold-and-white, art-deco Gatsby-inspired wedding cake. Jionni and I held the knife and made the cut, and then confetti snowed all over us. That was a total surprise. First we were on the magical cloud, and then we were in a beautiful blizzard. We kissed in the confetti and I just felt so happy and blessed that Jionni—a fling, this guido I picked up at the club, didn't even know his name and could barely remember having been with him the morning after—was the father of my babies and my soul mate. How crazy is life? It just proves that you never know what's going to happen to you, even while it's happening, if that makes any sense.

When my roomies and I fist pumped to Taylor Swift's "Shake It Off." I was thrilled to have my old *Jersey Shore* roomies at the wedding. Jenni is my BFF and we do everything together, including pregnancies (she gave birth to Meilani two months before I had Giovanna), and making fools of ourselves on TV. Sammi and Deena and I are still tight. Paulie and Ronnie are like my big brothers. My wedding was a mini *Jersey Shore* reunion. We talked about how much things change, and how much they stay the same. We used to party at Karma until dawn, dancing to house music and drinking until we puked and passed out. Now we're old, hardly drank, and got tired at 10:00 p.m. Not that night, though. We kept going, and going, for hours.

When the after-party got underway. Most of the guests left at midnightish. And then the real party got started. Jason Kim, the designer I work with on my clothing line, and I made track-suits for my wedding party with the word "Gatsby" on the front. We all put on our comfy clothes and went nuts. That was the best part of the wedding for me, when I was doing shots and dancing with my friends, celebrating this momentous event with the people who know me best, and have been with me through thick and thin.

When it was all over at 4:00 a.m., Jionni and I snuggled in the backseat on the way home, and decided to make a Wendy's run in the limo. I'd been eating right and working out to look slim in my wedding dresses for months. Now that it was over, I gave myself permission to eat junk food, and couldn't wait to bite into a cheeseburger. But when we pulled up to Wendy's, it was freakin' closed! I was so pissed. We got home at 4:30 a.m., and made Hot Pockets, pizza bagels, frozen french fries, and tater tots, sat down at the kitchen table, and stuffed our faces with greasy crap.

I woke up at noon the next day, hungover. The first thing I did as a married woman? Took a shit. All the nerves and jitters—not to mention the Hot Pockets—just came out of me. It was a great way to begin my life as a wife—clean, clear, and unblocked from the inside out. I still felt hungover, though. So I thought, *What will make me feel better?*

McDonald's! Jionni, Lorenzo, and I drove over there and ordered the entire menu. Cheeseburgers, nuggets, fries, everything. I ate it all. Woo hoo! I can inhale the entire McD's menu in one sitting!

I felt awful afterward. So I thought, *What'll make me feel better?*

A pepperoni-stuffed calzone! Jionni found me making out with the huge calzone in the kitchen that afternoon, and said, "Whoa. My wife is eating a cow."

I stayed in a postwedding food coma for a couple of days. But then I got back to reality (real reality, not the TV kind), and started working out again. I gained four pounds on my wedding splurge. It was worth it.

Now What?

I'm a grown-up, a wife and mother. So what do I do now? Do I plan my funeral?

I'd rather plan another wedding. I want to do it again, mainly because the first one went by way too fast. It was eight hours long, but it feels like the entire day and night just went by with the snap of a finger. I tried to take mental pictures, and we've got the official wedding album, too. But I feel like I missed so much of it. The only solution is to do it all over again so I can remember everything.

I said to Jionni, "Let's renew our vows next year."

He laughed in my face. Okay, maybe it is too soon to do another extravaganza. But I'd love to throw another huge party in ten years, and make the marriage new again. I know that, especially after you have kids, the relationship gets old. Stale. You need to make it special again, have fun and wild out. What better way to do that than throw a huge, extravagant party?

Once a party girl, always a party girl.

A lot of people I know say that the best time in their marriage was their wedding day, and it was all downhill from there. They warned me, "The second you say, 'I do,' something changes." I can see how that could happen. Our wedding was spectacular, and that single day can't be beat. But a marriage is thousands of days. We made vows for our wedding, and that was all well and good. But to make sure our first day isn't our best, Jionni and I decided to make vows for real life, too.

Nicole's Vows for Real Life

I, Nicole, vow to you, Jionni that . . .

We won't bring up the past. No need to drag out our dirty laundry, and we definitely have a lot of it. We've survived some savage fights in our early days, many of them caught on camera while filming *Jersey Shore* and *Snooki & Jwoww,* like the time I got drunk and flashed my ass in Italy, or the time I got drunk and made out with a girl at a club, and the time I got . . . I'm noticing a recurring theme here. Maybe I should edit this vow to be . . .

I won't get drunk. I mean *really* drunk. I don't think this is a concern. I lost my taste for alcohol—and my tolerance. I used to be able to go all night. At my bachelorette party in Atlantic City, I was destroyed after three drinks and ready for bed. I passed out long before my guests. I don't think I could do serious drinking damage anymore, even if I tried to.

We will bicker. As you know, you piss me off all the time. That's normal, I feel. People fight. If you don't fight, it means you don't care. So, I'll go ahead and get mad, and open my mouth when I have something to say. If I cause the fight, I'll admit when I'm wrong, and apologize. If you, Jionni, cause it, I'll forgive you for being such an asshole. Then we'll flush the whole fight down the mental toilet.

I will stay in a good mood. I believe that, when you're depressed, you bring your partner down with you and, as a couple, you can get stuck down there. The negativity leaches on to the relationship, which should be a source of joy. So, I vow to stay in a good mood, as much as possible, to lift each other up. If I'm not feeling it, I'll just fake it until I make it.

We will be idiots. You have to have fun, and for us, that means being goofy and silly. You see this quality in any longtime couple. They crack each other up. They're best friends and just enjoy hanging out together. They don't take each other, or themselves, too seriously. So, when you play with Lorenzo's toys and land a remote-controlled toy helicopter on my head that messes up my hair, I will laugh. And we'll make a habit of running around the house shooting each other with Nerf guns in the brain, pretending it was the Zombie Apocalypse. Heh. That was fun.

I'll keep surprising you. I will make some effort to be interesting and fun for you. After years together, things might get predictable. So I will throw you some curve balls to surprise you. Like last week, I cleaned the entire bathroom. It was sparkling. You came home and thought I'd been replaced by an alien.

I'll compare you to asshole ex-boyfriends, in a good way, only in my head. Everyone has a soul mate, and you, Jionni, are mine. I went through a lot of losers to get to you. I laugh (and cringe) looking back at how I thought I was in love with some of them. Whenever I get mad at you, I remember how much smarter, funnier—and sexier—you are than any guy from before, and I will fall in love with you all over again.

I will threaten *Misery* on your ass. As I've told you, we are never getting divorced. If you try to leave me, I'll tie you to the bed and break your ankles, and then you won't be able to leave because you can't walk. When I tell you this, you look at me like I'm crazy and we laugh. What's funny is that you think I'm kidding. When I say, "You're stuck with me. We're going to die together and be buried in a double casket," it's just a gentle reminder that you are mine for life. There's no escape, so you better get used to it.

I won't talk about every freakin' thing. I don't want to hear every tiny thing you do, think, or feel. And I'm sure you don't want to hear every detail of my shit, too. I mean, come on. We'll always share the big stuff, and the medium stuff. But the teeny-tiny stuff?

I'll keep the mystery alive by keeping that to myself.

I will walk away. During those times when I can't stand you and you can't stand me, I will go into my closet, close the door, and scream. We're not going to gain anything by being annoyed, so it's best to step back and get away from each other. We'll take a moment and be by ourselves. And then, before long, I'll get bored and lonely and want to hang out with you again.

I won't look for deeper meaning if there isn't one. We fight about stupid things, like doing the dishes. You get mad I'm not as good a cleaner as you are. It just doesn't matter. A friend told me, "If you fight about the dishes, it's not really about the dishes. It's about something deeper." I thought about this, and tried to figure out the deeper meaning of our fights, and came up empty. There just isn't a deeper meaning to every little thing. When you stop trying to go deep, you don't create problems that aren't there to begin with.

We will take stuff out on each other. We both get stressed. You have your ATM business that you're trying to get going, and all the logistical problems that come with that. I have my Etsy store, and so many orders that I have to stay up till all hours of the night getting my products done. We're both working as hard as we can to pay for this huge house we built and support our kids. The pressure builds up, and sometimes, a person just needs to scream. Instead of taking stuff out on others, we do it to each other. If you need to yell at someone, better it be me than your business partner, and vice versa. We won't take it personally, of course, because it's not.

We will agree to agree. I don't like the idea of agreeing to disagree. There'll always be some resentment left over. Instead, we'll agree to agree and try to see each other's side of it. This shouldn't be too hard. We're different people. Opposites attract. I'm outgoing and crazy, and you're reserved. But we are on the same page about the important stuff, like how to raise our kids and where to live, what to buy, where to travel, and what we hope to accomplish. We share political and religious views, and root for the same teams. In general, in a marriage, if the two of you don't agree on core values, it's not going to work. The rare times we do have a disagreement, we will come up with a compromise we agree on. For example, you didn't want to film our wedding for *Snooki & Jwoww*. So I promised you it would be the end, the last time cameras came into our personal lives, and we agreed to do it. If you didn't say yes, we wouldn't have.

We will live it, so we don't have to say it. We used to say "I love you" all the time, remember? But now, we're an old married couple and hardly ever do. Needing to hear the words, I feel, comes from insecurity. I used to be insecure, and begged you to say it. Now I'm not insecure, and don't care if you say it or not. In a way, saying "I love you" all the time is like trying to convince yourself it's true. You knows you're the cheese in my macaroni, and I'm yours. Love is understood.

Jionni's Vows for Real Life

Hi, this is Jionni, Nicole's husband. I like all of her vows, although she's lying when she says she doesn't need to hear "I love you." When she's away and we're hanging up the phone with each other, if I don't say it, she screams at me. So I'll edit that one vow of hers to be the first on my list . . .

I will say "I love you" when we hang up the phone, or I can expect to get torn a new asshole.

We will have kids, and be kids. We'll always try to have fun, and I take clues from our kids on how to do it.

We will lower our expectations. I mean about romance. As you know, Nicole, we're not very romantic. On Valentine's Day, we went for an overnight in Atlantic City and made it special. But on a daily basis, we're not the rose petal on the bed and champagne popping, edible chocolate underwear kind of people. As long as we both don't expect cards and flowers and all of that bullshit, we're good.

We will do time. I run a business part-time now. We spend a lot of time together, probably more than most couples now, but when my business is full-time and you travel for work, we can't. So when we are together at home, we'll stay close, play with the kids together, and just take advantage of the time. You're a good kid. I like hanging out with you.

We'll also take advantage of our breaks. If you're gone for three or four days, it's like a little relief. I got the kids to myself, and nobody is telling me what to do. The next day, though, I get the chance to miss you. When you come home, it's like new again.

We will ride out the dry spells. We are in one right now, actually. Most nights, I sleep with Lorenzo and Giovanna sleeps with you in our bedroom. So that's how it's been and how it's going to be for a while. But I can handle it. Nicole wants four kids, so I know we'll have sex at least two more times. I have that to look forward to.

You will yell, and I will listen (sort of). You can be loud. You know this. When we used to fight in the basement at my parents' house, I had to tell you to be quiet. But in our own house, you can yell and scream all you want, get all your stuff out. I'm not a yeller like you, but believe me, I hear what you say and I try to make it right.

We will fight about the small things. People fight, it's inevitable, I agree. We don't really fight about the big stuff; most of our arguments are over little things, like dishes. I like that. In a marriage, how bad can it be if all you fight about are the dishes? So I vow to go ahead and fight about these small things. It takes the edge off. If there are clothes on the floor, we yell at each other; it's just a joke, just another way to talk.

I will look for the good. I'll have to look hard . . . just kidding, jeez, relax, Nicole. Everybody has ups and downs in life, but you have to look for the good in each other. If you look into the good things, it takes you out of the bad. You just got to look for the positive angle, and move forward.

I won't think about the bad. I could talk about things that happened four years ago but I don't. If you think about bad memories, you can't put them behind you. Obsessing about past mistakes, from years ago or yesterday, won't get us anywhere. You can't change it, so we'll deal with it in the moment, and then forget about it.

We will save our money. I know you like this one. Things are good for us now financially. You have a lot going on and my business is taking off. One day, I'd like to earn enough so you can stay at home with the kids. But in the meantime, let's remember that we don't know how it's going to look in five years. So I vow to keep a close eye on spending, and you do, too.

We will remember that it's our marriage, not anyone else's. Nicole, you know I never asked for any of this, living in public, being on TV. I'm a low key guy, and I'm glad that part is over for me. I've learned to just ignore it. Before I met you, if anyone picked on me or called me names, I would fight back. But since I met you, I had to learn to ignore all that and know that none of that has anything to do with us. We know who we are. We know how we live. Let's just keep having fun and laughing.

Isn't he the best? I think back on my snookin' for love days, and can't believe I found him. It's like discovering a diamond in the Dumpster. For all of you single boo boos who have been looking and coming up empty, don't let losers get you down. I strongly believe that every single one of us has a soul mate. It might take a while, going through a battalion of pricks, dicks, and losers to find him. Looking back, I'm glad I made out and hooked up with all those jerks in my teens and early twenties. I don't think of them as failed relationships. They were steps on the ladder I had to take before I could reach Jionni. And then, my relationship with Jionni itself was a series of steps to get to where we are now—in a perfectly imperfect marriage.

A while back, when I was single, I kept a list of all the traits I hoped to find in a man. He had to be romantic. He had to have a last name that ended in a vowel. He had to be juiced up. He had to love his mom, but not be obsessed with her (FYI: It's totally fine if Lorenzo is obsessed with me; whoever he brings home one day better get used to it). I wrote down all these qualities in my pink journal, and prayed that a man who'd fit the list would walk into my life. But now that I've been with the love of my life for four years, and married to him for four months, I know that everything on my list doesn't really make a difference in our day-to-day lives. He fits the profile, but what really makes Jionni the cheese in my macaroni is just one thing, and one thing only:

When he looks at me, I see it all in his eyes. Love, trust, a mischevious sparkle. It's all in there. Even when he's mad at me, or annoyed, or frustrated, I see it. When you can just look at your man, and know that he adores you no matter what, that he's there for you no matter what, it's everything.

So when your soul mate comes along, you might not recognize him right away. But eventually, one day, you'll be talking to him, or arguing with him, and you'll look in his eyes and you'll see exactly how much he cares about you. I can't quite describe the look or how you'll recognize it. Trust me, though, you'll know it when you see it.

CHAPTER TWO

Strong Friendships

With the major exception of Jwoww who I met six years ago (it feels like I've known her forever), my BBFs are people I've loved since way, way before I got famous—before I could tie my shoes or get my own juice.

HERE'S STEPHANIE

Nicole and I have been best friends since we were three years old. We met in preschool. When I got there that first day, I was crying and clinging to my mom's leg. Nicole came over to me, and gave me a giggly pen from Nickelodeon. It was a really cool pen, and I let go of my mom's leg and started playing with Nicole. My mom must have thought she was leaving me in good hands, and she slipped off. Nicole and I have been best friends ever since.

The majority of Nicole's close-knit friends—including about half of her seventeen bridesmaids—came from preschool. Even though we met so long ago, we're still a tight group twenty-four years later. We're family. We've gone our separate ways, but once or twice a year, we all get together for dinner or a trip. Last year, we all went to Las Vegas and had a blast. This year, we were at Nicole and Jionni's wedding.

I know it's unusual for such a large group to stay so close for so long. Nicole has been the glue, which is even weirder considering her life. How many of us have a childhood friend who went on to become famous? In a way, I always knew something like this would happen to her. She had an outrageous, fun personality and was always the center of attention, even back then.

My old friends have proven, time after time, that they're there for me. I know if I need them, they'll drop everything, get in a car or on a plane, to be with me, and I would do the same for them. We've all matured. It's not the same as it was in high school. Back then, we showed loyalty by kicking in an enemy's car door or egging a rival's house. Simpler times. Our problems are more complicated now, but the loyalty hasn't changed at all. Whatever happens, we'd die for each other.

I can't imagine myself without them. As Stephanie said, we're all spread out, all over the map, in different states. Each of us is in a committed relationship, but not all of us have kids. It doesn't matter, though. When we get together, we're just ourselves, just the girls who made friends with each other on day one of preschool. It's possible we haven't grown apart because we're really shallow and aren't deep enough to change. We *are* the same people we were growing up, the same bunch of idiots.

HERE'S MOM

Hello, this is Helen, Nicole's mother. It's not so surprising to me that Nicole is still close with her preschool friends. They have a strong bond that's been reinforced by all of the families. It's a blessing to have friends you've known your whole life, and I'm grateful for it. Each one of these girls is like a daughter to me and a sister to Nicole.

As an only child, Nicole always wanted a sibling. Her friends were as close as you can get to having sisters, and, like real sisters, you stick together through thick and thin. They have been in and out of my house for decades. We've spent holidays and vacations together. Nicole's friends have brought me as much joy as anything else in my life. The wedding was like a family reunion, me with all my daughters. It made me so proud to see the two full tables of Nicole's preschool friends, now with their boyfriends and husbands.

When they were little, they weren't always adorable, though. The sleepovers made me crazy. I remember endless nights, the girls talking and laughing until dawn. In high school, they were always getting into trouble, and doing things they shouldn't have been doing. All those shared experiences have bonded them together. The partners-in-crime mind-set just stuck.

How lucky are we to have each other's back all this time? It's like a miracle. But luck isn't the only reason we've stayed so close. On *Jersey Shore*, we used to talk about the Girl Code, the rules of conduct we uphold to support each other in our dealings with dudes. I think there's an unspoken Girlfriend Code, too, the rules of conduct we uphold to maintain a friendship. The first and most important rule is that you trust each other. If any of us had repeatedly violated the trust, then it'd be hard to be loyal to that person. None of my preschool friends have sold me out, or been shady. You hear stories about reality stars' former friends selling stories or photos of them to the gossip magazines. None of mine have ever done that. I could tell them anything and they'd never repeat it to anyone. We make each other feel safe. If you can't trust a friend, then there's no reason to be in the relationship. That sounds cut-and-dried, but life is short. As grown-ups, we have careers, kids, and men in the picture. It's hard to keep up friendships. For one to survive, you have to make an effort. I'm not going to pour time and energy into something that doesn't really matter to me.

HERE'S STEPHANIE

Throughout our lives, Nicole and I and all of our friends went to Midnight Mass together on Christmas Eve with our families. We also spend part of the holiday driving to each others' houses and exchanging gifts among our families. It was our tradition. My boyfriend now has a hard time adjusting to the fact that we spend Christmas going house to house to visit my childhood friends and exchange gifts with friends, and then we all go to church in a huge group. He says, "I don't get it. They're not even your family."

I tell him, "They are my family." Nicole is my sister. Helen is my second mother. At the wedding, I gave her a hug and said, "Hi, Mommy." When my mother saw Nicole in her gown, she burst into tears because Nicole is like her daughter. Just because we're not blood doesn't mean we're not as close, closer, than someone you share genes with.

Another Girlfriend Code is that you genuinely give a shit about what's going on in your friend's life. It's a lot easier if you have things in common. I'm so glad Jenni is a mom now so we can talk about pregnancy and baby stuff. (We're hoping our daughters will be next-generation besties. If it turns out that Meilani and Giovanna hate each other, I have no idea what Jenni and I are going to do.) Both being parents, we relate to each other on a new level about the most important part of our lives right now. I can tell her in vivid detail about how Lorenzo threw up in the car, and how I had to scratch puke out from the crack in the seat and how, two days later, I still have vomit flakes under my nails. It's surprising that not too many people want to hear such stories. But Jenni and I think this is hilarious, and tell each other all about our sore nipples and black-hole vaginas.

For the most part, thank God, my friends have progressed from their drunk slut years to being responsible women with boyfriends or husbands and careers at the same pace as I have. Even if we didn't grow up together, though, we'd still have one majorly important thing in common to keep us close: a long history together. We're all invested. We were there at the beginning of our life stories. We'll be there the whole way through, just to see how it ends.

Back in school, Stephanie and I had this notebook we used as a shared diary. I'd start the day with it, and spend all of algebra class writing her long notes about what I was thinking, like how much

I wanted to set the teacher on fire, or what the boy I had a crush on was wearing. The whole class would go by while I scribbled away, page after page, in the notebook. To the teacher, it must have looked like I was taking down every word he said.

In the hallway between classes, I'd pass the notebook to her. She'd spend the whole period writing a note about what she was thinking, and responding to what I wrote earlier. At lunch or whenever we had free time together, we'd read through the day's notes, clarifying points and adding to them. If, for whatever reason, we couldn't get time together to go over the day's entries and talk about them, it was really hard. Like, agony. My life, thoughts, and emotions centered on that notebook. Stephanie's, too.

We shared *everything.* If a thought went through my head, I wrote it down, and she did the same. No wonder we were addicted. When you are literally living inside someone else's head, especially such a cool mind as Stephanie's, you don't want to leave. We didn't pay much attention in class. I tried to multitask and do both, but most of my brain was in the notebook. Incredibly, we were never caught by a teacher or had the notebooks taken away. It would have been really boring for anyone else to read the excruciating details about what we ate for breakfast, and how it felt when a certain boy glanced at us, and how his hair looked and how he smelled. Thank God they were never stolen by other girls or by a boy, or you wouldn't be reading this book right now because I would have died of embarrassment.

I like to think Stephanie and I invented texting way before smartphones. Notebooking.

Exchanging our thoughts on paper like this went on *for years*. We filled a hundred of those spiral notebooks. Stephanie still has piles of them in her house. Sometimes we look at the notebooks, and shake our heads at how stupid we were about everything we wrote. It was all about who looks cute, what we were doing that night, who we could get to buy us beer. With hindsight, though, I see our entries as the early history of our friendship. Steph and I have our notebooks. Jenni and I have our TV shows. Our histories are recorded. We don't need the documentation to remind us why we're close. But it's nice to have the notebooks and the shows to remember the little things and to look back and laugh at it all.

It wasn't always sunny with me and Stephanie, though. We got in fights all the time—including kicking and slapping. Back in high school when emotions ran high, it didn't take much to get pissed off. We'd get furious with each other and wouldn't talk for a few days. Usually, we kept up with notebooking, though. But one time, I didn't pass the notebook between classes. It was like going cold turkey on vodka. But I was so mad at her—I can't for the life of me remember what the fight was about—and refused to let her in my head. Stephanie wanted nothing to do with me, either. We ignored each other for a month. And then, one day, while in math class, I just started writing a note, not about our fight or anything deep, just same old bullshit about boys and clothes. When I saw her in the hall, I gave it to her, and we picked up right where we left off. When your friendship is as thick as ours was—and is—one fight could never end it. The story had to keep going.

We still get mad at each other, and I'm still in that high school mentality when I get pissed sometimes. Jenni and I had an argument recently, and I reacted by ignoring her e-mails and refused to like any of her Facebook posts, even pictures of her daughter. That was brutal! I didn't yell at her or exchange tense e-mails. I waited until we were face-to-face to talk it out. Don't fight with friends by text! You don't want evidence of saying something you regret later on. When you're in the same room, you're never as mad as you can be when you're alone with your phone.

HERE'S STEPHANIE

Nicole and I rarely fight. When we do, it's pretty big. One fight, we didn't speak or look at each other for a month. Then, one day, we met in the hallway at school and just hugged. That was it. We never talked it out. We didn't have to. There wasn't any bad blood between us because we were always honest. Sometimes, you just need a little space. We took it, and then we hugged and that was it.

I couldn't possibly list all the things Nicole and I have

been through together over the years. Whenever life was hard for me, she was at my door. A fight with my mom? Problem with a boyfriend? She always managed to pick me up and make me laugh. She's still doing it. If I'm feeling down about myself, she says, "Screw them. You're beautiful. You're perfect. I love you." It's the best thing a girl can have, a friend who believes in her.

❤ ❤ ❤

So back in preschool where I met my crew, I was obsessed with glitter glue. I still am, to tell you the truth. I'm crafty, meaning, I love arts and crafts, and actually have a room in my house devoted to making stuff. I even have an Etsy store, called Nicole's Craft Room. One of my best-selling items was a mug that said, "You're the Jwoww to my Snooki." When I first designed the mug, I posted a photo of it on Instagram. I initially spelled "you're" wrong. It read, "Your the Jwoww to my Snooki." The grammar police corrected me. So thanks, Internet, for making me look stupid! Typos happen, people, even when you're (not your) using a Sharpie.

Anyway, my point is, Jenni and I, our friendship, has become something bigger than the two of us. It's been compared to Lucy and Ethel, Laverne and Shirley, Edina and Patsy on *Absolutely Fabulous*, just two idiot broads who get in trouble together, have crazy adventures and laugh the whole way through. Hey, we shoot our breast milk at each other. You can't get closer than that. I take one look at Jenni's face, and laugh my ass off. It's the biggest compliment you can make to a friend: "Your face cracks me up." I'll probably put it on a mug one day. When Jenni and I are both senile, living in a nursing home, wiping drool off each other's faces, and sexually harassing all the young male nurses, I know I'll wet my Depends from laughing hysterically whenever we make eye contact.

It's hard to believe that when Jenni and I met at the shore house in Seaside five years ago, she didn't like me. I liked her, but she wanted nothing to do with me. Then I got punched in the face in a bar one night. Jenni said watching that moment brought up feelings she didn't know she had and she realized how much she cared about me. I'm glad I got punched in the face because it brought Jenni and me together. We've come a long way since then. We've traded sleeping with vodka bottles to sleeping with our babies. We're not peeing behind the bar at a club, and are now peeing behind the fence in our own houses.

Now, I'd give her a kidney if she needed it. I'd wrap it up nice in a box and hand it to her. From that bumpy start, our lives have become interconnected. We're linked together in millions of minds. How did two random people become such great friends? I'd call it destiny or fate. We were just meant to be. Not just me and Jenni, though. Everyone in the *Jersey Shore* house was meant to be together. We became a family over the course of one summer. No one can really understand what it was like to be on that show except the eight of us.

The intensity of shooting is how we got so close, so fast. We had cameras on us 24/7, and we weren't allowed to make unnecessary contact with anyone back home. It was really stressful to be so isolated in that bubble, so we relied on each other to make it through. There were many days when I said, "Dude, I don't want to do this today," but the camera was in my face, filming everything. We were all dealing with and feeling the same things, and it helped us to bond. I don't want to compare it to a war, but we relied on each other to pull us through it, and to make it out alive and in one piece. You don't forget a closeness like that. You can't, even if you wanted to.

Even though I don't talk to a few of the cast members, we have a once-in-a-lifetime connection because of our experiences in Seaside Heights, Miami, and Rome. If they really needed me, I'd be there for them, too. Most of us have stayed close and are in each other's lives. The last season aired a few years ago. Since then, we've all settled down. Most of us are in committed relationships. A few of us have kids. It seems like forever ago, but season one of *Jersey Shore* aired on MTV in 2009. We've done 180s, and become totally different people than we were then. Or, I should say, the same, just evolved. From chimps to humans in just six years.

♥ ♥ ♥

New Best Friends. You just click and it feels like you've known someone forever. Sometimes, making a NBF blows up in your face. You feel like you can trust this person, and you share all your secrets too soon. You really don't know this person you confided in, and then, after one fight or weird moment, she stabs you in the back. It's not pretty.

I don't make new friends so easily myself. It's not that I'm suspicious and untrusting. I'm open to people coming into my life. I've made incredible friendships in the last few years. But I do keep my guard up. Although it seems like I'm 100 percent an open book because I've been filmed for years and have shown my life on television, I'm actually kind of shy about revealing my deep inner self to new people. I'm not ready to dive into something on a first, second, or tenth meeting. There are exceptions, though.

HERE'S JOEY

This is Joey, Nicole's pet Bear. We met just a few years ago. I'm a makeup artist and I was hired to work at an online TV show sponsored by MAC Cosmetics. It was a Halloween competition. Nicole was the host of the event. Anyway, I did the models' makeup and met Nicole that day for the first time. We got to talking, and something in our personalities just clicked. Then we started working together, and became close friends. She brought me on Snooki & Jwoww, and now we're doing the Naturally Nicole podcast together.

I think of Nicole as a well-rounded friend. She's great for going out and wilding, and having the time of your life. But she's also nurturing when you need it. When my mom passed this summer, she dropped everything to be with me. We were supposed to start filming a scene for Snooki & Jwoww, but Nicole told the producers it would have to be delayed until I was ready. She and Helen, her mom, sent huge baskets of fruit and sandwiches, beautiful flowers, and cards to my parents' house. She came to the wake and was so supportive about everything and made sure I was doing okay. All of my relatives loved having her there. She's very close with my family now, like I am with her parents and Jionni's family. Her support was really touching, and it was so instrumental to my getting back to my old self after the loss. I'm just so grateful to have her in my life.

It's all about family to her. She didn't have a big family growing up, so she's created a giant family of friends. People stick with her because she brings you all the way into her world. She's incredibly generous with friendships and she wants all of her friends to be friends with each other. Her impulse is to include everyone, which is why she brings *people on her TV shows, and always gives shout-outs on Twitter and Instagram to people she's working with. I've been doing makeup for a long time. I've met plenty of celebs who are selfish about their fame and never share it with anyone. Nicole is the least selfish person, let alone a celeb, I can imagine.*

Joey and I did hit it off right away and we've gotten closer and closer as we pile on the shared experiences, many of them seen on TV. A deep friendship grows over time, and then you can't imagine not having that person in your life. It can't be rushed or forced. It has to happen on its own, like you're not even trying.

I have lost a few friends over the years. Some people come into your life, and then they flow right out of it. I've distanced myself from people I just don't have anything in common with anymore. Life is short, and I don't have time to feel awkward when I see or talk to them.

Some of my childless friends don't get why projectile baby poop stories are so entertaining. They want to talk about a night they went out, got wasted, and gave a guy a blow job in a taxi. Five years ago, I would have been all ears. But now, these kind of stories make me feel like we're not living on the same planet. I get it, not everyone is fascinated by stories about my childbirth and how I shot a placenta across the room. But it's more than just the divide between who has kids and who doesn't. Once you have kids, you realize there is so much more to life than partying. Even if I didn't have kids, I don't think I'd still be going out all night long anymore. I wouldn't organize my life around getting drunk and smutting with strangers in clubs. Can you imagine what I'd look life if I hadn't changed at all since my early twenties? It'd be pathetic! The great divide, for me, is between the people who grew up and the ones who didn't. I grew up. I want to spend time with other grown-ups, even if we act like stupid kids sometimes.

You don't need a million friends. You just need one person to confide in—and that person can be yourself. If I need to talk to Steph and it's too late to call because she has work in the morning, I will just talk to myself in the mirror. In my head, I talk back. I have actual conversations with myself, which makes me clinically insane. I think it's healthy, though. If I need to work something out, I know I can do it by myself, with my multiple personalities. One of them, let me tell you, is a class A bitch! But I never stay mad at myself for long.

Here's a typical conversation I have at night, when I can't sleep:

Me: *I can't sleep. This blows.*

Other Me: Stop complaining. Why is everything such a drama with you?

Me: *I'm not complaining, I'm just saying. I've got a lot to do tomorrow.*

Other Me: Blah, blah, blah. All I hear is bitching.

Me: *You're [not your] such a bitch!*

Other Me: Look who's talking.

Then I (we) crack up and I feel lot better about having insomnia. Jionni has woken up to find me giggling in our bed at 3:00 a.m. He says, "What's so funny?" He thinks I'm clinically insane. You probably do right now, too. I might be crazy, but I'm also never alone. Think about it.

Other times, I talk to myself to figure stuff out, like what I'm going to do with a free hour. It's so rare, I don't know what to do with myself.

Me: *Should I go shopping or get my nails done?*

Other Me: How about both?

Me: *Sounds good, you greedy whore.*

Other Me: Mwah, love ya.

Getting my nails done is an excellent idea. Why didn't I think of it myself? LOL.

Other times, I work out my emotions by screaming at my face in the mirror. The mirror is your friend. It's got nothing to do with how you look. I can't always cry with other people, but if I look at myself in the mirror, I can burst into tears. Wait, that didn't sound right. It's that I feel free to let it all out when it's just me and my reflection. My cry face is hideous—squinty eyes with a huge double chin. When I see how ugly it is, I start to laugh. I make myself sob, and then I make myself snort. I'm like my own "I laughed, I cried" movie that takes place, from beginning to end, in the bathroom.

CHAPTER THREE

Strong Body

When it comes to getting fit, I've heard that knowledge is power. The theory has it, that the more you know about how the muscles develop and the best exercises to make that happen, the stronger you'll be. The only problem with the "whole knowledge is power" thing: I'm a total idiot.

Guess what? It turns out I don't need to know what an amino acid is. I've been working on my body for the last few years, and have transformed it from soft and cubby into a hard and muscle, without one iota of understanding about how it's happened.

What is even more powerful that knowledge? Going to the gym every day. Kicking my own ass until it hurts. You might not have to do that to be fit, but I do. I wasn't born with a perfect body like Kendell Jenner. She would probably look sensational no matter what she does. And we've certainly see her from every conceivable angle with every possible body part zeroed in on. All celebrities, especially the Kardashians, are scrutinized about their size and shape. How many millions of hours and pages of newsprint have been devoted to discussing the extraordinary bootadiousness of Kim K.'s butt? Probably more than were used covering the last presidential election (or maybe that's just in the media that I pay attention to).

Poring over celebrity body parts is just the nature of the beast, and it sucks. I think the reason my changes have been so closely monitored is that I've never been shy about showing myself at my worst. For the first few years of my being on TV, my naturally short, squat body was seen in all its glory. Season by season, I got fatter and fatter. People got used to thinking of me in a certain way. They called me an Oompa-Loompa, a basketball, a bowling ball with a wig. Looking back at photos of those times, I cringe. I really was round. On a short stack like me, every pound really shows around the midsection, and mine was plump as hell.

Then I met Jionni, and we got serious. I wanted to be a sexy, fit girlfriend, and actually got in pretty awesome shape for two months there—until I got knocked up with Lorenzo, and my slim, strong shape went to shit. I didn't exercise during my first pregnancy. My attitude was, this is the only time in my life when I can just eat whatever I want. I gave myself permission to shovel pasta into my pie hole. I ate like an ox and got as big as a whale. In fact, if you put an ox on a leash and walked it in front of me, I might've tried to eat it. On the last season of *Jersey Shore*, filmed during a hotter–than–Death Valley summer when I was seven months pregnant, I was huge and miserable, living on the beach, sweating gallons with gigantic boobies and zit villages popping up all over my bloated body. So sexy.

After I gave birth and waited the requisite six weeks postpartum, I hit the gym again, determined to get back in shape. My motivation was to be a fit mom, so I could carry Lorenzo, a diaper bag, and his stroller, up and down the stairs to the basement. Unlike before when I lost weight and got in shape for Jionni, doing it for Lorenzo was both easier and harder. It was easier because I had powerful motivation to do it for my son. It was harder because it took so long to see results. I was working out with my trainer, Anthony Michael, six days a week and eating carefully prepared meals for six months before the scale budged. I know now that the numbers weren't moving because I was gaining muscle while I was losing fat. Once most of the fat was gone, my new muscles emerged, and my weight dropped. I lost forty pounds of baby weight, and had never been stronger or felt better in my life.

I spent most of my first pregnancy, self-wetting, creating life, and turning to lard on the couch. I resolved not to let history repeat itself during my second pregnancy with Giovanna. I changed the game plan. I ate right and hit the gym nearly every day, including the day before I went into labor. I wound up gaining only twenty pounds, thirty less than I put on with Lorenzo. I lost most of the weight within days of giving birth, and could fit into my jeans after only two weeks. You bet your ass I tweeted about it. I was proud! I worked hard to bounce back that fast.

I am woman! Hear me rawh!

Yeah, it seems unbelievable, which is probably why there were so many rumors that I had plastic surgery or took pills. One article reported that I ate nothing but egg whites and that my friends were staging interventions to stop me from becoming anorexic again, like I was briefly in high school. None of it is true. I got in shape the old-fashioned way: By sweating balls.

Being fit and fabulous is like having a superpower. It makes me bullet proof. Feeling raw power course through me is so much cooler than partying and smutting. Running a seven-minute mile is the ultimate drunk. What can I say? I'm hooked on being a badass. I don't care what I look like when I'm doing my thing. At the gym, I'm not a wife, a mother, or a pseudocelebrity. I'm just flesh and bone, muscle and blood. I'm in my body and in the moment—and there is no better feeling in the world, even when my thighs are on fire. Cardio keeps me sane. It's the off switch for stress. I float out of the gym, knowing I can handle all the stuff I have to do every day as a wife, mother of two, brand designer, podcaster, and master crafter. If I weren't in great shape, I couldn't function. Being fit makes my life possible.

The best part about physical strength: you can always get faster, stronger, tougher. There is no limit to how tough you can get; there's always one more push-up, one more mile, one more pull-up to do. Unlike dieting, which makes you weak and is bound to fail, exercise always works to clear your mind, reset your stress, and strengthen muscles. Every push-up is yours to keep.

HERE'S JIONNI

I don't really care how Nicole looks or how big her muscles are. I love her regardless. But I do care about her mood and how she acts toward me. When Nicole is working out a lot, she's a much nicer person, and much easier to live with. When she's not going to the gym, she picks little fights, and gets in a bad mood. The number one rule of our marriage is to have fun together, and her working out is a big part of making that happen.

When I don't work out, I get pissy. Jionni knows to duck when I come into the room if I miss a training session. Exercise is my Prozac. It smooths out the rough edges and makes life's annoyances easier to take. I work out for Jionni's sake as well as my own, to be a sweeter person for him.

I do NOT work out to be skinny. Skinny is not my goal, and it's not really in fashion these days anyway. My goal for 2015 is to gain ten pounds of muscle. Why bulk up? I know I'll feel the surge of power, and I'll be able to accomplish so much more in life, as well as lift a double stroller with one finger. I need to be able to carry heavy boxes of supplies up two flights of stairs to my attic craft room, without needing help from Jionni. I can unscrew any jar, no matter how old and how crusty. Just try me. Bring a jar of pickles to any of my appearances. I'll sign it, *and open it* for you.

My body transformation didn't happen overnight and I didn't do it alone. After my son, Lorenzo, and my husband, Jionni, the most important man in my life is my trainer, Anthony Michael. We get together three times a week so he can torture me, and listen to me grunt like a tennis player taking a poop. He's seen me leak all kinds of fluids. Mainly sweat, but also pee. I was seventh-months pregnant with Giovanna, doing squats, sneezed, and that was it. A trickle down the leg. Fortunately, gym mats are easy to wipe clean.

People have said online, "Of course, Snooki can lose weight. She has the money and the time to hire a trainer and spend hours a day at the gym." First of all, you don't need to hire a trainer. I work with Anthony because he's my guru and I like having someone push me. If you don't have access to a trainer or the money to hire one or even join a gym, no problem! You can push yourself and work out at home in no more space that the size of a yoga mat—and you don't have to buy a mat, either.

Or you can just go take a stroll for an hour which doesn't cost a penny. My friend Perez Hilton told me he lost thirty pounds just by walking for an hour every day, and he wasn't so fit to begin with. Now he's a supercut rock star. If you live in an apartment, you can run up the stairs—or just take the stairs instead of the elevator. If you have a computer, you can look at workout videos online, like the series on my blog called Workout Wednesdays.

As far as the line that I have all the time in the world to work out, no. Why do people think I've got all freakin' day to spend at the gym? I've got two kids, a husband, a house, a weekly podcast, a book to write, and a handful of brands to manage. Sometimes, I'm in the city from 5:00 a.m. to 9:00 p.m. doing meetings. By the time I get home, the kids are asleep. Even on those long days, I make sure I do crunches or squats in my room, just to do *something*. Also, it doesn't take hours a day to get fit. According to Anthony, if you do the right exercises the right way, you don't need more than fifteen minutes a day to get in shape and lose weight. (I've included a breakdown of his daily fitness techniques in a few pages.)

On some days, I can't find fifteen minutes, though. Like all working moms, I feel rushed and under the gun to get everything done. So how do I squeeze in a workout? I make it a top priority. It's way up there on my list. It's not down at the bottom, the thing you do after every other chore and responsibility has been met. I'd rather let ten loads of laundry pile up than miss a workout. So what if the house is a mess and the sink is full of dishes? If I don't work out, I feel like crap. I'd rather feel like Superwoman in a messy house than a piece of shit in a clean one.

How many hours of TV do you watch? How much time to do you spend on Twitter? If the answer is "more than an hour a day," then you have time to exercise. Saying you don't have fifteen minutes to devote to fitness is a poor excuse. You're being lazy, and you know it. How am I so sure? Because I used to make a million excuses, too. I'd go to bed every night, and my last thought would be, "Tomorrow, I'm going to the gym and run five miles and lift weights." In the morning, I'd come up with ten reasons why it was impossible for me to do it. Usually, the reasons were bullshit, like I felt sick (hungover) or had someplace to be (the bar), or just that I felt too comfy on the couch and didn't want to suffer. Running was agony back then. I hated it, so I avoided it like the plague.

It's a proven fact that working out gives you more energy. Back in the day, when I was lying in bed until noon, I had no energy and felt horrible about myself for being fat and lazy. I'd get out of bed bloated, and cry in my closet because nothing looked good. I'd think, *I hate my life.*

Since I made the change, I get up earlier (the babies help a lot with that), and push past any reluctance or laziness, and go to the gym anyway. Now I had tons of energy. I'm not bloated. My clothes look hot, which puts me in a positive mood, and makes me a better wife and mommy. I think, *I love my life.*

The key to change hating your life to loving it: Don't give yourself permission to be lazy or treat your body badly.

Why do we do that anyway? If your ass could talk (farts don't count), it would say, "Get offa me!" I think women don't do what they know is good for them because of self-sabotage. Not to get too shrinky-dink about it, but I believe we sabotage ourselves because, on some rotten, scummy level down deep, we don't think we deserve to be happy or that we're capable of reaching our goals, so why try?

Every single woman deserves to be happy. Every woman can be ecstatic with her life, care for herself, and do whatever will make her feel strong and fit. Love yourself in an active sense. Get offa your numb ass, and do what you know will turn your body and brain around. Anyone can build their muscles and superwoman their body. Anyone, regardless of age, fitness level, and athletic ability. You don't need to be an ex-cheerleader or a jock to get fit. You just need that first day when you say, "No more bullshit" and get yourself moving.

How to Kick Ass

Anthony Michael gets a lot of credit for transforming my body and the way I think about fitness. He's a busy dude. Despite having a gym to run, a meal delivery service (check out his menus at anthonymichaelfitness.com; I eat his meals every day), he carved out a few minutes to talk to me about the secrets and science of improving your body.

When we did this interview, I wore my glasses and a cute hat and took notes with a pad and pen, like a real reporter.

Nicole: Hi, Anthony.

Anthony: How's it going, Nicole?

Does it matter what time of day you work out? Like, if you don't have time in the morning, is it just as fat-burning to do it in the afternoon?

It really depends on your own body, but generally, to get your metabolism going and keep it going all day, it's best to work out in the morning. You kick-start your metabolism to burn fat all day. If your schedule is crazy, like yours, or if you're not a morning person—like you; when I ask you to come in before 10:00 a.m., you moan and groan into the phone—the next best time of day to work out is after work but before dinner in the 4:00 to 6:00 p.m. range. That gives your body the opportunity to utilize your dinner macronutrients more efficiently to achieve your goals. Separating your weight training and cardiovascular workouts by several hours would be ideal.

For me, it's all about losing fat and gaining muscle. Is there a certain type of exercise that gets you there?

You have to choose what's right for you. Some people focus on weight training. Some are CrossFit nuts. Some just do cardio or are marathon runners. I believe you should do everything in moderation. For you, Nicole, to achieve your goals, I have you do a combination.

The foundation of training is weights. The average person—meaning, not a competitive athlete, just someone who wants a desirable physique—needs to increase muscle mass and muscle tone. Muscle controls metabolism. The more muscle you have, the faster your metabolism, which is the process of converting stored fat into energy. Muscle needs much more energy, so the more you have, the more fat you burn at a faster rate.

After doing a few sets of weight training on a specific muscle, you can trick the body into burning extra calories with plyometrics on that specific muscle. For example, you've been working out your leg muscles with weights. Before you move on to your core or upper body, do five minutes of explosive jumps that involve the legs, like squats, burpees, or box jumps. When you reach muscle fatigue, move back to weights on the next muscle group.

Cardio is the last piece of the puzzle. I have you do high-intensity interval training, or HIIT. The goal is to get the heart rate up to its maximum for twenty to thirty seconds. Then you get to rest until you're breathing normally. Next, you go again to your max for thirty seconds, and recover again. Forcing your body to get up to maximum heart rate really fast not only burns calories, but it develops toner muscles. I don't recommend the treadmill for HIIT. It takes too long to get it up to speed. I prefer sprints outside. If someone is in decent shape and has been cleared by her doctor, I start her at four reps—getting to maximum heart rate and recovery—and working her way up to twelve reps. You can do all the cardio you need in just ten to fifteen minutes a day.

A lot of people do long, slow-paced cardio after weight training. But there's evidence to show that walking at a steep incline for forty-five minutes, for example, turns off the mTOR protein synthesis pathway. When you weight train, you activate the pathway to gain muscle. The last thing you want to do is turn that off. I'm not saying slow pace cardio is bad for everyone, but it should be done at the opposite part of the day as weight training.

The mTOR . . . um, what?

The mammalian target of rapamycin.

Now you're just making shit up.

All you need to know is that if you want to gain muscle mass, doing long, moderate-paced cardio is not helpful. You can actually lose muscle mass by running distances. Look at Olympic sprinters versus marathon runners. The sprinters have big muscles and look powerful and strong. The marathon runners look slight and weak.

What usually happens, when training for a marathon, is that you increase your caloric intake slightly. You eat more, but not that much in comparison to the calories you're burning. Over time, with long, moderate-paced cardio, the body learns to burn fewer calories for the activity you do. In other words, you do more and burn less.

When you do HIIT and combine sprinting with weight training, the body learns to burn more calories per the activity you do. You train the body to burn more by doing less. As a result, you get a desirable, lean, toned physique faster.

Now, it all depends on what you want to accomplish. I know people who have strong, desirable physiques who can lift a car but can't run a mile. I know people who can run five miles and can't unscrew a jar of pickles.

I can! Any jar. Try me. But what you're saying sounds upside down. I've heard my whole life that

to get strong, you have to run long distances.

I know it sounds crazy to most people, but you actually lose muscle mass by running long distances. The body requires amino acids, which are the building blocks of protein. For muscle and the collagen in your skin, you need protein. For cells in every vital organ to repair and regenerate, you need protein. For your brain to function, you need protein.

The brain is very smart. If you're not eating enough protein, it goes looking for some in your body's stores of it. So where does the brain go to get amino acids to keep functioning? The very last thing on your brain's priority list is muscle mass, so it's the first place it goes to get protein. If you go out for a long run without the proper nutrients, your body will consume the protein in your muscles and leave the fat cells alone. You keep the fat, lose the muscle, and slow your metabolism. Marathon runners need to consume a ton of protein, or lose muscle mass. Considering the distances they go, and the carbs for energy they crave, they can't possibly consume enough protein.

Also, that kind of cardio activity stresses out your adrenal gland, releasing cortisol, the hormone that makes you hold on to belly fat. During our evolution, back when we were cavemen, our bodies learned that stored fat is essential to prevent starvation during stressful times like a winter's famine. When we go through stressful situations now—not famine, but traffic and deadlines, for examples—the body releases cortisol and sends the signal to your cells to hold on to fat. Running distances is stressful. Your body thinks it's running from a saber-toothed tiger. Cortisol is released, again and again, resulting in adrenal fatigue. You're exercising too much, not eating enough nutrients to replenish the demand.

But marathoners are skinny.

Skinny, with stamina and mental toughness. But they're not strong the way you want to be, with powerful, visible, toned muscles in your arms, legs, and behind. If you want a desirable physique, which, to us, means lean, toned, and strong, long, medium-intensity cardio is not going to do it. To achieve your goals, you don't need hours of pounding the pavement and racking up miles. You only need thirty minutes of a combination of weight training and HIIT.

Speaking of which, here's your . . .

WEEKLY WORKOUT PLANNER BY ANTHONY AND ME

If you bought this book when it came out in October, you're about to enter into the fall holiday season and winter hibernation time. You'd rather sit in front of a fireplace with hot chocolate than go to the gym. I don't blame you! It's hard to get motivated when you're bundled up in a cosy sweater. BUT—summer bodies are made over the winter. I want to help you guys get that bikini body! If you want a perfect booty, these workouts will help you get it. All you need are some hand weights, like 3- or 5-pound dumbbells, and some space on the floor. Anthony and I came up with fast and furious workouts for you for six days of the week. You don't have to do every single one. If it seems like too much, just do three days a week at first. Soon enough, you'll be hooked and push yourself to do more. You'll see.

Monday: Lower Body

Booty call! Squats are not the most fun to do, but they really work your leg muscles and lift that butt up. I feel the burn after twenty seconds of doing them. The pain is worth it, though. Squats are the best way to get that Kardashian curve. According to Anthony, they're the most basic compound lower body exercise, meaning, doing this simple movement for pretty much everything below the waist.

Basic Squats

1. Stand with your feet a little wider than shoulder-width apart, toes slightly pointed out.
2. Arch your back with your head and chin up.
3. Put your arms out in front of you at a 90-degree angle, parallel with the floor and with your palms facing down.
4. Come down by bending your knees and sliding out your butt until your thighs are parallel with the floor. Always keep the pressure on your heels, never your toes.
5. Come up to the standing position, nice and quick.
6. After a set of fifteen, rest and recover, or until your heart rate is at 50 percent capacity. To calculate that number, subtract your age from 220 and divide by 2. For example, I'm 27, so 220 - 27 = 193. One hundred and ninety-three is my maximum heart rate. My recovery heart rate is half of that. So you divide 193 by 2 to get 96. I start my second

set when my heart rate is back to 96. It usually takes about a minute to come back down. If it takes longer for you, just wait until then.

7. Do four sets of fifteen reps or sixty squats total. It should take less than 10 minutes.

ADVANCED OPTION: To increase the intensity, add some weights. If you have a barbell, great. Put it across your shoulders, milkmaid style. Drive through the downs and ups, focusing on the muscles that are contracting. Keep going until muscle failure—when you really feel the burn and your legs are so tired,

you think you can't go on—using the weights. Then put the barbell aside, and do a set without it.

CARDIO ADD-ON: Sprints. Go outside in the sunshine (lots of vitamin D to soak up out there). Run as hard as you possibly can, full-on sprinting, for 30 seconds. Then walk for 30 seconds or 1 minute until your heart rate is back down to normal and you're not gasping for breath. Then do another full-on crazy fast sprint for 30 seconds, followed by another 30-second to 1-minute recovery period. Do four to twelve reps, depending on your fitness level.

Tuesday: Upper Body

Call to arms—and chest and back. This series of what Anthony calls "upper body pull" exercises strengthen your biceps, triceps, deltoids, pectorals, and your entire back. Although we think a lot about getting that curvy ass and tiny waist, you have to build muscles all over your body to raise your metabolism and burn fat faster.

The following workout consists of three different exercises—Push-Up Rows, Front Raise Sequence, and Hammer/Kickback Combos—that strengthen these muscles. You do one exercise for 20 seconds straight, and then move on to the next one for 20 seconds, and then the next. It adds up to 1 minute of movement. Then, you get a rest until your heart rate goes back to normal, and then you do the sequence again, same order, same interval length. Repeat the pattern for ten or fifteen reps. It should take around 20 to 30 minutes.

Push-Up Dumbbell Rows

1. Start in the push-up position (aka plank position) on the floor with your hands holding 3- to 5-pound dumbbells (if you don't have dumbbells, you can do it without).

2. Staying in the plank position, bend one elbow straight up toward your chest, leaving the other hand as is. You're balancing on just the one hand, but try to keep your body from moving to one side. After the row motion, put your hand back down, and then lift the other hand, bending the elbow.

3. Switch back and forth, lifting one hand and then the other for 20
   seconds. Then move on to . . .

Front Raise into Lateral Raise
into Shoulder Press

1. Don't be scared. It sounds complicated, but it's not. First, the front
   press. Stand up with your feet hip-width apart. Holding the dumbbells,
   raise your arms straight out in front of you, knuckles up, until they're
   parallel with the floor. Then lower your back to your sides.
2. Next, the lateral press. Raise your arms straight out to your sides like
   Jesus on the cross, until they're parallel to the floor. Don't go above
   your shoulders. Then lower your arms back to your sides.
3. Last, the shoulder press. Starting with your arms at your sides, bend
   your elbows so your hands are next to your shoulders, and then lift them

straight up over your head.

4. Repeat the sequence (front, lateral, shoulder) for 20 seconds. Then move on to . . .

Hammers and Kickbacks

1. Again, it sounds way harder than it is. Start with hammers. With your arms at your sides, feet hip-width apart, bend your elbows like a classic bicep curl motion, but keep your hands with your knuckles facing out.

2. Then do kickbacks. Bend forward at your waist to a 45-degree angle. With your elbows still bent at 90 degrees, straighten your arms behind you, so they're parallel with the floor.

3. Do this combo for 20 seconds.

4. After completing a minute of this, rest until you've made a full recovery.

5. Do three reps if you're a beginner; ten to fifteen if you're an expert.

Wednesday: Total Lower Body

On Monday, you focused on the bootay. On Wednesday, you do your thighs, lower back, calves, and lower abdomen. This kills it for everything below the waist. Like yesterday, you'll do three exercises —Squat Jumps, Side Lunges, and Squat Thrusts—for 20-second intervals, and then rest before repeating it.

Squat Jumps

1. Standing upright with your feet shoulder-width apart. Hold a 3- to 5-pound dumbbell in each hand.
2. Do a vertical jump.

3. Come down from the jump into a squat position with knees bent, butt sliding out, thighs parallel to the floor, and head and chin up. Your arms hanging down at your sides.

4. Repeat vertical jumps into deep squats for 20 seconds.

Side Lunges

1. If you used weights in the previous exercise, put them to the side.

2. Stand with your feet together. Lift your right foot and move it to the side so your feet are now 3 feet apart.

3. Bend your right knee until your thighs are parallel to the floor. Your left leg is straight, and just going along for the ride.

4. Bring your feet back together.

5. Step out with your left leg, and then bend your knees until your left thigh is parallel to the floor. Twenty seconds of this, and then . . .

Squat Thrusts

1. Stand upright with your feet together.

2. Bend at your waist and put your hands on the floor in front of you.

3. Jump back with your feet into the plank position.

4. Then jump your feet back to your hands, and stand up.

5. You will be dying after 20 seconds of that.

But it's not quite over yet. I didn't mention one more sequence earlier. It's a real killer, and you probably would have wanted to skip this entire day if I told you about it up-front. But now that you've done the others, you can throw this one in, too. There's a method to my forgetfulness, I swear.

Forward and Backward Lunges

1. Get into the lunge position. Right leg forward, left leg back. Drop your hips and bend your right knee so it's parallel with the floor. Your left knee should dip to almost touch the floor.

2. With a quick hop, switch your legs so they're reversed. Drop your hips. Your left leg is bent, your thigh parallel with the floor. Your right knee is almost touching the floor.

3. Keep your left leg planted. Bring your right leg forward, and go into a lunge again. Then step backward with your moving foot and go low again.

4. Do a quick hop, to reverse your feet again. Twenty seconds of this.

5. Recover!

Beginners, do three reps of the sequence of all four exercises. Experts, do fifteen reps. The entire session should take about 10 to 20 minutes.

CARDIO ADD-ON: Sprints again. I know, they suck. But you only have to do half a dozen of them, and it takes only about 10 minutes. Remember the old saying, that you can do just about anything for 10 minutes. Half of your cardio time will be spent in recovery anyway. So it's really only 5 minutes of pain.

Thursday: Upper Body Again

Anthony calls these exercises "upper body pull," a complement to the pushing from earlier in the week. They target the chest, shoulders, and triceps. Same as before: You do each exercise—Walk-Outs, Push-Ups, and Dips—for 20-second intervals. When you've completed a series, you recover for a minute, and then start again.

Walk-Outs

1. Start in the plank position on your elbows.

2. Thrust in with your feet, and then thrust back out to the plank again.

3. Stand up.

4. Then go back down to the plank on your hands.

5. In the plank, go down to your elbows.

6. Repeat the sequence for 20 seconds.

Push-Ups

Either from the plank position or with your knees on the floor, do a push-up, as many as you can for twenty seconds.

ADVANCED OPTION: Explosive Push-Ups. When you come up, push so hard that your hands come up off the floor. It's not as impossible as you think. I can do one or two of these.

Dips

1. Back up to a chair or the couch.

2. Put your hands on the piece of furniture shoulder-width behind you.

3. Lower yourself so your legs are straight out in front of you, touching only your heels to the floor.

4. Use your arm strength alone to lift your body up and down.

Four sets of the sequence for beginners; ten to fifteen for experts. The entire session will only take up to 20 minutes. And you will feel it all across your upper body the next day, I'm telling you.

Friday: Total Bod

Now you can bring it all together and hit pretty much everything you've got in what Anthony calls "total body pull" exercises that get at your back, deltoids, biceps, abdominals, hamstrings, and glutes. I love Friday workouts because Anthony gave these moves some hilarious names:

Sumo Squats

1. Grab your dumbbells. Your arms start at your sides.
2. With your feet a foot wider than shoulder-width apart, toes pointed out, do a deep squat.

3. Then, while in the squat position, do a bicep curl.

4. Then lift your arms over your head.

5. Come back down to the intermediary place, and then lower your arms.

6. Straighten legs to the standing position.

7. Repeat for 20 seconds.

Dead Lifts

1. Stand with your feet hip-width apart, feet parallel with each other.

2. Bend your knees slightly.

3. Bend at your waist, sliding your butt out, letting your arms drop so the
   weights in your hands hang down.

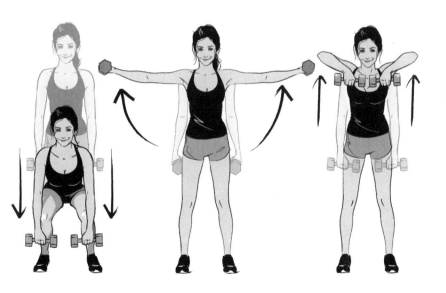

4. While in the squat position, do a lateral raise, followed by an upright row. To do a row, start with your arms hanging down in front of you. Then, lift your hands with the dumbbells touching straight up. Your elbows flare out to the sides. Lift the dumbbells to your chin, and then lower your arms slowly. Repeat for 20 seconds, and then move on to . . .

Superman Planks

1. Get onto the floor in the plank position.
2. Lift and stick your right leg out behind you.
3. Lift and stick out your left arm in front of you at the same time. Hold for a couple seconds.
4. Then do the opposite right-left combos.
5. Switch back and forth for 20 seconds.

You know the drill: do the whole sequence between four and fifteen times, depending on what you can take.

Saturday: Plyometrics

For the first weekend day, you're going to break a serious sweat doing plyometrics. It's like aerobics with explosive moves, designed to get at your core and pretty much every other muscle in the body. Plyometrics spike your heart rate quickly, which, in turn, makes your muscles grow and increases your metabolism. It's a serious workout, not just playing around, although that's what it feels like. Don't forget to drink a lot of water when you do plyometrics, before and after.

Stars

1. Start in a squat position.
2. Explode up in a lateral jump with your arms raised high over your head,

stretching your body as high as you can. Try to touch the ceiling.

3. Repeat ten times. Do five to ten sets. You will die.

Squat Thrusts

1. The usual torture. From standing with your feet shoulder-width apart, bend at your waist and put your hands on the floor.

2. Kick out into the plank position.

3. Bring your legs back.

4. Stand up.

5. Repeat ten times. Do five to ten sets.

Marches

1. Stand in front of a solid box or low table.

2. Touch the bottom of one foot on the top of the box. Then jump to do the other foot. It's like running with your legs lifting higher than usual. It's a way to run in place, with maximum benefit.

3. Take your time until you get the rhythm right and then speed up.

4. Do it as fast as you can for 20 seconds and then recover.

5. Beginners should do sets of five; experts can do all day.

Sunday: Rest and Relax

Family day! Just have fun. It might mean taking a long walk around the neighborhood, or hanging at the playground, or hiking with friends, doing a yoga class, or sitting on the couch watching a *Walking Dead* marathon. You worked hard all week and deserve to chill in whatever way you want. You can restart your fitness routine again on Monday. Rest is just as important as working out, so six days on, one day off, is a necessary part of your fitness routine.

That was my problem before. I had it in reverse, one day working out, six days sitting on the couch. Glad I got that sorted.

Slammin' Preggers Workout

When I'm pregnant—which I hope to be again soon—guess what? I still work out! There are so many benefits to exercising while being knocked-up. You can carry all that weight a lot easier when you've got muscles. You increase your blood flow, extra important to make sure the baby gets everything he or she needs in there. Since your organs shift around and get squeezed because of the giant uterus pushing against them, you need to make sure each part is getting all the oxygen it needs. Exercise guarantees it. If you're anything like me, and you turn into a psycho bitch from the hormonal flood, working out turns you back into a human (for the most part). It's not an exaggeration to say that exercise saved my marriage when I was pregnant with Giovanna, because otherwise, I might've torn Jionni's head off when he annoyed me.

When you're a whale, it's not easy to motivate yourself off the couch, let alone get your bloated fat ass to the gym. But it makes a huge difference to your health, the baby's health, and your attitude. As I've said, I didn't work out with Lorenzo, and I gained forty pounds, felt like shit, and hated looking at myself naked in the mirror during the pregnancy and for months after. With Giovanna, I worked out nearly every day. Giving birth wasn't easier (the pelvic floor muscles, the one muscle group I didn't pay enough attention to: kegels!), but I felt lighter and more like myself from day one. I lost most of the weight after two weeks. When I was given the go-ahead from my doctor to get back to the gym after six weeks, I picked right up where I left off and felt as slim, sexy, and strong as ever.

Anthony works with a lot of soon-to-be mommies. Here are some of the benefits of exercising while expecting:

- You keep your muscles strong, and that usually means an easier delivery. (Says him!)
- Exercise relieves pregnancy-related back pain and headaches.
- It increases circulation to the extremities, which can be a problem. (So true. My first pregnancy, my feet and ankles were so swollen, I couldn't wear my shoes in the third

trimester. Not a tragedy, but very sad.)

- Working out increases overall functionality, from walking down the street, climbing stairs dancing, or just standing to chop veggies for dinner.
- It gives you a sense of well-being, which is so important when you are carrying another human in your belly.
- It maintains muscle mass during pregnancy and will help you bounce back after giving birth. (This was too true for me. With Lorenzo, it took six months. With Giovanna? Six weeks. Big diff.)

The intensity of your preggers workout depends on what you feel you can handle. Even a small amount helps. The positive effects are immediate and real for you and your baby. There are some precautions, of course. Talk to your doctor about them, and clear your exercise program with him or her, just to be safe.

Anthony's "Don'ts" for pregnant ladies:

- Don't let your heart rate go above 140.
- Don't do any exercise on your stomach.
- Don't do any exercise on your back.
- Don't do any exercise that puts pressure on your abdomen.
- Don't exercise in a hot and humid environment. You want to keep your body temperature stable.

- Don't forget to drink water! Stay hydrated before, during, and after a workout.
- Don't go overboard. Choose a dumbbell weight you can easily execute fifteen reps with without struggle. If in doubt, go lighter.
- Don't do any routine unless you've consulted your doctor first.

To strengthen the core muscles—everything between your knees and your chest—the best overall workout while you're pregnant is everyone's favorite . . .

Planks

1. Get into plank position with your forearms and toes on the ground.
2. Go up from your elbows to your hands.

3. Hold for 5 seconds and then go back down to a forearm plank.

4. Hold for 5 seconds, and go back up onto your hands.

5. Repeat process for 30 seconds, and then stand up to recover fully for up to 60 seconds.

6. Do ten reps.

Side Planks

1. Get into the side plank position, up on your right elbow with your right hand on the floor in front of you. Keep your left arm at your side. Your feet are stacked, with the outer edge of your right foot on the floor, and your left foot resting on top.

2. Contract your abdominals to hold the position for 15 seconds.

3. Switch to the other side and keep squeezing those abs.

4. Check your heart rate. If it goes over 140 after one side, take a rest and wait until your heart rate is under 100 to switch sides.

5. Repeat fifteen to twenty times, depending on your fitness level.

Cardio, too? Uh, yeah. You can bounce around with a bun in the oven. Your baby is safe in there, thanks to the shock-absorbing amniotic fluid and the muscular walls of your uterus. It's like a panic room for your baby. Anthony had me do intervals on the treadmill. I didn't run too fast, though, to keep my heart rate between 120 and 140. I'd run at 5 or 6 MPH for 1 or 2 minutes to get my heart rate up, and then slow it down to 3 MPH during recovery periods for 1 or 2 minutes. In total, I'd be on the treadmill for around half an hour. For beginners or those in later stages of pregnancy, you can get your heart rate up to 140 by walking on the treadmill with a steep incline and then lower it during rest periods.

You won't regret the sweat, boo boos. I'm so glad I kept up my fitness the second time around—and I'll do the same for the third and fourth (and fifth?) times, too. You can stay fit, even when you feel like shit. (I think I'll embroider that on a pillow and sell it on Etsy.) In fact, I'd say do it *especially* if you feel like this. Just 5 minutes of movement can bring on a positive attitude adjustment and prevent you from murdering your husband. Exercise saves lives, people! Not only your own.

CHAPTER FOUR

Strong Motivation

As the saying goes, "You get abs in the kitchen, not the gym." The gym gets your head on straight, and makes you feel accomplished. It grows muscles, and speeds up your metabolism. But if you're not eating right, or eating too much, you won't drop the flab. For weight loss, diet is priority number one.

If you've followed my career, you know that, in the past, I never missed the opportunity to have a few margaritas or scarf a platter of nachos. But I've come a long, long way from my Age of Gluttony, and have completely changed the way I eat and drink. The biggest change in my eating habits has been mental. I think about food in a different way. Food is still a source of pleasure. I love what I eat. But, even more than flavor or taste, I love what good food does to my body. It gives me all the vitamins and nutrients I need to grow muscles, and have enough energy to chase two kids around the house.

HERE'S JOEY

In the old days, when Nicole and I did events in Las Vegas or Los Angeles, we'd get bombed at a club, and then come back to the hotel and order room service. Pizza, chicken wings, french fries, nachos. We'd go through the menu and order only the greasiest, cheesiest food. A rolling cart loaded with horrible food would arrive at 2:00 a.m. We'd wake up the next day and find empty plates all over the place. Nicole would be in bed, still drunk, with chicken bones stuck to her face.

She's a late sleeper, especially after a booze and junk food binge. Waking her up to get her dressed and made up for work in this condition wasn't easy. I'd brushed the crumbs off her face, straddle her on the bed, and do her makeup while she was still asleep. Then I'd get her into her outfit for the day—it was like dressing a life-size rag doll—and basically carried her into the car, and arrive at the event barely on time. We've had some close calls in the past.

Those days are long over. Nicole is dedicated to her health right now. Before she got her trainer, she'd drink sugary cocktails and eat late at night. Since Lorenzo, she doesn't drink any soda and orders red wine when we go out.

She eats well, too. At home, she gets the prepared meals from Anthony. They're all superbasic food, nothing too complicated, but she tells me they taste good. Jionni is the cook of the house, and he's making family recipes that are fried and have a ton of cheese. If he makes his mom's famous lasagna, or deep-fried cutlets, Nicole has just a taste, and then eats the healthy stuff.

Even on the set of Snooki and Jwoww, with tables full of sandwiches and junk food, she has salads and fruit. I've tried to get on the healthy bandwagon. Nicole is encouraging me to see Anthony for training sessions. She's a cheerleader for fitness in real life and pushes everyone she knows to get fit because it's made her really happy and she wants her friends to feel the same way.

Thanks, Joey, for reminding me about food orgies I didn't even remember in the first place. Nice visual, by the way. Me, drooling drunk on a pillow with a buffalo chicken wing glued to my cheek. Oh God.

Welp, he's right. That used to be me. I didn't care what I ate, or drank. If it was fried and smothered with cheese, I'd eat it. No wonder I had no energy and couldn't get out of bed until 2:00 p.m. Gross. I feel slimy and tired just thinking about that—and constipated. Junk food blocks you up so bad. I switched from cheese to veggies, and from soda to GTL (green tea lattes), and now my pooping is like clockwork.

Fans ask me where I find the willpower to resist greasy, fatty food I used to gorge on. To me, it's not a matter of willpower. Willpower—when you use all your mental strength—doesn't last. You get really tired fighting against your impulses all day long. I think this is why diets don't work. You just get worn out and exhausted from trying to muscle up willpower, and then you just hit a wall. When you've got no strength left to resist, you say, "Fuck it," and go wild on a pizza.

You can't rely on willpower. What is reliable for the long term? Motivation. My motivation comes from looking at the faces of my babies. I want to be here for them until I'm one hundred. You can't live that long on a soda and cheeseburgers. Jionni motivates me, too. When we make eye contact, and I see love and passion reflected back at me, I want to make sure that look never goes away. Not that he wouldn't love me and want me if I gained fifty pounds. He loved me when I was Godzilla huge while pregnant with Lorenzo. But I feel sexier in my own skin when I'm toned and fit. The love and passion reflected in his eyes is my own confidence. The worse feeling in the world is when I think I'm a fat blob, and that Jionni is wondering, "Why the hell did I marry her?" It might be the farthest thing from his thoughts. What he thinks doesn't matter as much as what I think of myself. And then I wonder if he's thinking the same thing. It's a crazy, dysfunctional loop that I don't ever went to get on again. It won't happen if I have a salad instead of a pizza.

I love my kids. I love husband. I love myself. So I eat salad.

Yeah, it's that simple.

If you have motivation—to live long, to be sexy for your man, to keep your head screwed on right—you don't need white-knuckle willpower at all. You're not fighting yourself to do what's good for you. You're doing what's good because you have a list of good reasons.

It's easy to say, not always easy to do. In the days of waking up with a pile of greasy plates stacked around me on the bed, I believed I loved myself. But I didn't practice it. It was an idea, not a lifestyle. Motivation to eat right has to become a habit. It doesn't happen overnight. At first, you might feel deprived, like you're denying yourself Doritos and beer. That stage lasts, on and off, for a month. Eventually, you don't want junk anymore. If you make mindful, healthy choices over and over again, it becomes automatic. After three months, you come full circle. Eating junk feels like you're depriving your body the healthy food that makes you feel great.

I do fall off once in a while. Planned cheats are actually a good idea. The fact is, ice cream tastes freakin' amazing, even it if it makes you blow up like a blimp afterward. You can't be on a strict diet *all* the time. At my wedding after-party when all my friends were pigging out on french fries, not joining in would have been boring and stupid. We were all having fun and laughing and eating the greasy stuff. I'm not saying peer pressure made me do it. In certain situations, if you know you'll feel sad if you don't indulge, then go for it with awareness and a clear conscience. I knew it was for a special occasion and I gave myself permission. I was mindful about making unhealthy choices, just as I'm mindful about the healthy ones. Plus, if you plan the cheat, you don't have guilt. Guilt sabotages any diet.

During the summers when we live at the shore, Jionni, the kids, and I walk to the ice-cream stand. Once a week, I get myself a cone. I do it for my kids as much as for my own pleasure. I don't want Lorenzo or Giovanna growing up thinking, "Mommy doesn't eat ice cream. There's either something wrong with ice cream, or wrong with her." Ice cream is *great*—once in a while. So I have it, once in a while. If I didn't indulge now and again, I know myself, I'd obsess about it. Same thing goes for wine. It's great on occasion, not so great if you drown in it. Moderation is an excellent motivational strategy. When I'm in Los Angeles doing press, and the kids won't see me, I might even have one cigarette if I'm in the mood. Then I come home, I don't touch them.

Having a little sugar is as human an urge as breathing, shitting, and fucking. So give in to it, just don't over do it. Plan your cheat moments in your iCal or write them down. "On Saturday night, I'm having a steak!" and then go have it. If it's on the book for Saturday, you have that to look forward to all week, and you'll probably be careful with calories until then. I can't stress this enough: do not try to be perfect, or you are fucked. Whenever I hear a woman tell me, "I stick to my diet to the letter," I know it's not going to last. Perfectionism in a diet—in everything—is the enemy of success.

Why does perfectionism even exist? We're only human. We're bound to screw up. You have to be kind to yourself and forgive yourself for your faults. Especially on a diet, women are too hard on themselves. You're not a bad person if you eat a so-called bad food. What matters is how you react to it. Do you forgive yourself, laugh about it, and eat healthy at your next meal? Or do you feel awful, cry about it, and in your self-hatred, give up on healthy eating entirely?

Do what I do. Laugh at yourself, really hard, and then have a salad.

Usually, my cheat meals are something yummy that Jionni or my mother-in-law, Janice, makes for Sunday dinner. I look forward to it all week, and get really excited to take that first bite. The all-time fave for the LaValles is Janice's Lasagna. It's a multistep dish, and kind of hard, but totally worth trying.

JANICE'S LASAGNA

Serves 8

BASIC SAUCE

Olive oil

3 garlic cloves,
  chopped

1 yellow onion,
  chopped

4 cans (28 ounces) whole peeled
  and blended tomatoes

Salt and pepper,
  to taste

1 to 2 bay leaves

1. Coat the bottom of the pot with olive oil.

2. Sauté the garlic and onion for 1 minute.

3. Pour in the blended tomatoes.

4. Add salt and pepper to taste.

5. Add bay leaf and simmer for 2 hours.

6. Remove the bay leaf.

FILLING

1 container (15 ounces)
  ricotta cheese

1/4 cup Parmesan cheese,
  grated

While the sauce is cooking, make the filling. In a medium-size
bowl, mix the cheeses together, adding salt and pepper to taste.

CONSTRUCTION

1 box (16 ounces) no-boil
   lasagna noodles
Basic sauce (see above)

Filling (see above)
12 ounces mozzarella
   cheese, shredded

1. Preheat the oven to 350°F.

2. In an 11 x 18 Pyrex pan, ladle a layer of sauce.

3. Then put a layer of noodles on top.

4. Next, a layer of filling, about 1/4 inch thick on top of the noodles. Sprinkle a handful of shredded mozzarella on top of that.

5. Add sauce again.

6. Keep layering—sauce, noodle, cheese—until you get to the top of the pan.

7. On the very top, add one more layer of noodles, sprinkled with mozzarella.

8. Bake for approximately 40 minutes or until the cheese bubbles.

9. Stuff your face. Salud!!

How to Get Motivated

Some Dos:

Do ease into it. Change doesn't happen overnight. If people are overweight and they go straight on a strict diet, it's not going to work. You need to take it slow. The first week, just think about what you're eating and how, if you were dieting, what you would eat instead. I get it, you want to drop three sizes overnight. It just doesn't work that way. But if you take it easy, and pace yourself, in a few months, you'll be a lot happier with your size.

Do make small substitutions. Instead of frying, start grilling. Instead of beef, eat turkey. You can eat the same meals, but make them with one healthier ingredient or cooking method. One of my trainers still eats cookies but she substitutes coconut oil for butter. It's one step in the right direction. One step leads to another, and another, and before you know it, your cookies will be sugar-, gluten-, and saturated-fat-free. So next time you want a cheeseburger, have a turkey burger instead. Instead of french fries, have sweet potato fries, and eventually, go for a baked sweet potato. If you crave pizza, get it with whole wheat crust, and eventually, substitute it with a mozzarella, tomato, and basil salad. Grilled chicken substitutes for fried chicken. Grilled zucchini instead of fried. You don't sacrifice taste at all. Just sprinkle your grilled food with a little salt, drizzle it with a little olive oil, and you'll be fine.

Do it for the right reasons. Dieting to please a man or to fit into a certain size or to look like a celebrity won't get you far. But doing it to feel good about yourself and to get healthy and to be fit for your family will keep you on the right track.

Do look for inspiration in people you know. A lot of people have told me via social media that they've struggled with weight loss, but kept at it because they know my story. I've heard so many times, "If Snooki can do it, so can I." It's absolutely true! Take inspiration where you can get it. If it's from me, I'm honored. If it's from a friend or a relative, or a girl at work, great. Don't be jealous of others' successes.Be inspired by them and learn from their example. Look at them and think, *One day, that's going to be me.*

And some Don'ts:

Don't expect instant results. There is no pill you can take, no quickie surgery to grow muscles. Even liposuction takes weeks of downtime to heal. Instead of spending $10,000 on a tummy tuck and then waiting three months for the swelling to go down, you can walk for an hour and eat your veggies for the same length of time, get the same result, and not spend a penny. Trendy diets won't melt fat overnight, no matter who endorses it. You have to ask, "If any one of all those diet books that promise instant, permanent weight loss actually worked, why are there a million others?" You have to work to get a great body. When you finally achieve your goals, you feel pride down to your newly slender toes. The pride is what I'm addicted to. The great body? An amazing side benefit.

Don't get discouraged. It took me a year to get fit and lose all my weight from Lorenzo. *A whole year.* For those first six months when the scale didn't budge, I was tempted to say, "Donezo," and console myself with milk shakes. That moment, when you're frustrated and ready to quit, is like a test. If you can get through that plateau, you'll be rewarded for it. So don't let a setback knock you off. Keep going, and something wonderful will happen.

Don't weigh yourself. During those six months of not seeing the scale move, I was gaining muscle while losing fat. Muscle is heavier than fat. Even though I felt stronger, the number on the scale didn't move and I freaked out. The scale is bullshit. What matters is how you fit into your clothes. You can be the same weight but if you replace fat with muscle, you'll look better. If you need a way to measure your progress, use that one pair of jeans. You know the one I mean. Try them on once a week to keep you honest.

HERE'S MOM

I'm proud of Nicole for how well she eats and her focus on health and nutrition as opposed to being skinny.

During high school, she was obsessive about eating, and did have a problem with anorexia. She pushed herself to an extreme and got carried away with losing as much weight as she could. It was a big cause for concern for her father and me.

As a mother, it's not easy to watch your child struggle with something like an eating disorder. Her father, Andy, and I started paying close attention to what she ate and talked a lot about the health consequences of having only a cracker a day. How she'd get weak, and that her organs would stop working the way they're supposed to. Every day, we had a conversation about how her day went, and we asked her a list of questions, such as, "What did you eat today?" and "What were you feeling at the time?" We were always trying to get to the real reasons she felt she shouldn't eat. She says she had to be as small as possible to keep her spot as a flyer on the cheerleading squad. I believed it ran deeper than that. She was under a lot of pressure with cheerleading and some social situatioons. Boys, fights with friends, partying. I think it got to her. I felt that if I could help her get to the core of what was bothering her, it would relieve the anxiety she was having. This process of talking and listening went on for about four months until whatever pressure she felt to lose weight let up. She calmed down and started eating normally again.

I'm not surprised Nicole has become an inspiration for other women about healthy eating and weight loss. The high school anorexia and the few other times since she got carried away about weight taught her how to do it the wrong way—starvation or trying fad diets that promise instant results. When she got serious about her health after Lorenzo, she was determined to do it the right way— by exercising and eating a lot of vegetables. Her hard work has paid off.

There have been magazine articles that say she's anorexic again. She's in the public eye, and it is kind of incredible that she could look so slim only a few weeks after giving birth to Giovanna. But having been there when she was anorexic, it's ridiculous to even suggest that the way she lives now is anything like she did back then. She eats three meals a day, with snacks. During her eating disorder, she ate nothing. Ice cubes, a grape, all day.

The only similarity I can find between those two periods of her life is determination. Nicole watched what she ate throughout her second pregnancy because she had a wedding

What to Eat

Yum, I love my food! Every bite I eat is delicious and exactly what my body needs. It's important to say that everybody is different. I can only tell you how I eat and what works for me. It might not be the right diet for you. It wouldn't hurt to talk to a nutritionist about your own body's needs.

Since Anthony Michael makes most of my meals (not him personally; he has a food delivery service that I order most of my meals from), I'll let him give you the big picture.

HERE'S ANTHONY

For Nicole, whether she's eating one of my meals or something she makes herself, every breakfast, lunch, and dinner should be lean protein plus healthy fats. She has a single serving of chicken, turkey, fish, or eggs with as much green veggies as she wants, and a drizzle of olive oil, coconut oil, or an avocado with her salad.

Nicole's two postworkout meals (a protein shake immediately afterward, and a snack an hour later) should contain the majority of her carbohydrate intake.

The protein shake is made of powdered whey protein, a single serving of simple sugar (fruit), and a serving of a complex carb (like oatmeal). Why that combo? When you exercise, your muscles burn glycogen, which are stored carbohydrates. For the muscles to recover, you have to replace the glycogen with a combination of simple sugars, like berries and apples, and a complex carb, like oatmeal. To grow and repair muscles after a workout, you need a quick-digesting protein, too, like whey powder.

One hour postworkout, be it a snack or a full meal depending on when she does her workout, Nicole should have a lean protein source plus a complex carbohydrate. The perfect meal then is, for example, a baked sweet potato and grilled chicken, or a bowl of brown rice and a piece of broiled white fish. You can sauce it up with lemon juice, soy sauce or mustard. Just stay away from sugary sauces like ketchup and BBQ, and use healthy fats like olive and coconut oil instead of butter and margarine. Keep it lean, no fatty meat when eating carbs.

With the exception of the postworkout shake and meal, I don't go crazy about when people should eat. It's a good

Can I just say, I am addicted to the postworkout protein shakes
Anthony makes. They're my reward. The whole time I'm working
out, I keep myself going by thinking, "When this is over, I get a
shake." Anthony makes them fresh at the gym. But if you don't go
to a gym or they don't have blender, you can make them yourself.
Put one serving size of protein powder, a banana—or an apple, or
a cup of berries—1/2 cup of oatmeal, and 1/2 cup of almond milk
into a blender. Pour into a glass and enjoy. You can buy protein
shakes, but be careful what you get. A lot of companies aren't legit,
and put all kinds of junk in their shakes.

HERE'S ANTHONY AGAIN

*There is just so much bad information out there about
how to lose weight and gain muscle. Most people in the
fitness industry talk about the one method that works for
them alone, which is why you and a friend can do the same
thing and only one of you loses fat. Low-carb diets might
be helpful to some people. But, especially if you work out,
your body needs carbs to function. If you don't supply*

your brain and muscles with glycogen, they'll consume themselves to get it. Carbs are essential to increase muscle mass. This is good news to anyone who loves fruit and whole grains.

I am a trainer, but I do make nutrition an important part of my training and my business. I'm an advocate of personalized nutrition. The cookie-cutter approach, as in one diet fits all, is wrong. A lot of people in the diet industry say you have to do Atkins or vegan or low-carb. Not me. I've worked with people who did well on low-carb, and others who succeeded with other plans. The only universal rule is that no eating plan works unless you can stick with it. I've found that a plan that encompasses a lot of different ideas is the most effective. When people like their food, they have a better chance at success. So I start with the basic plan and then incorporate different foods and habits once I see how you respond and keep altering it as you go.

Before you start any regimen, talk to your doctor or trainer about what your body type is, and what your nutritional needs are. Don't just buy a book that overpromises and applies to all people. You're not all people.

Anthony's Dos and Don'ts for Weight Loss

It's easy to stay motivated when you love what you eat and have a guru like Anthony to explain the whys, keeping the reasoning as simple and delicious as the meals themselves.

HIS DOS (IN HIS WORDS):

Do count overall calories. *It's popular to say, "not all calories are the same" in the nutrition world these days. It's absolutely true that one calorie of broccoli has a different impact on your body than one calorie of butter. But overall calorie consumption is still the number one concern for weight loss. No matter what you eat, if you eat too much or too little, you'll hit a plateau or gain weight. It's not necessarily practical to count every calorie, and there will be days when you go over. As a general rule of thumb, the average size women should aim for 1,500 calories per day for weight loss, and to moderate as your weight decreases. When Nicole was at her highest weight right after she had Lorenzo, she weighed 140 and ate 1,400 calories per day, with a minimum of 1,000. She might not have counted calories, but I did for her. If she went below 1,000, her body would think it was in starvation mode and would hold on to fat to survive. As she lost weight, we worked her calories down to 1,100. Now, as she's maintaining her weight, she's eating between 1,050 and 1,200. Keep in mind that Nicole weights one-hundred pounds.*

Do control your carbs. *When anyone eats carbs, their body releases insulin. Some people are insulin resistant or what I call carb sensitive, meaning, they don't get the quick energy from carbs, but immediately convert sugars into fat. If you're diabetic or prediabetic, you're definitely carb sensitive and should closely control intake. I never tell people to eat zero carbs, though. Everything in moderation, closely moderated.*

Do carb cycling. *The body requires carbs to grow and maintain muscle mass. Carbs are essential if you want to be toned and get strong, but you still have to be careful about when you consume them. My preferred method, what I used with Nicole, is called carb cycling. The basic method is to take in carbs postworkout only, specifically after weight training. No matter what time of day you work out, that's when you should load the majority of your carbs. All other times, keep carbs low and you'll lose body fat and maintain muscle mass in the process.*

AND HIS DON'TS:

Don't randomly eat sugar. *Believe it or not, simple sugars are an okay choice, but* only *postworkout. That's the only time you want the body to spike insulin. The best way to do* *that is with high-glycemic foods like fruit and certain veggies like beets and carrots. Low-glycemic foods like brown rice and whole grain bread slowly bring up insulin. When your muscles are pumped, you want a quick spike to release the nutrients straight to the muscles. Some body builders use real sugar, even candy. For someone who wants to lose weight, use fruit instead.*

Don't combine fat and sugar. *This combo packs on pounds fast. It's the worst possible combination for weight loss. Ice cream. Chocolate bars. Eat rarely.*

Don't drink soda. *It's not only full of calories, its got chemicals and dyes that rob your body of nutrients, vitamins, and minerals. If you're addicted to bubbles, switch to seltzer. Nicole gave up soda for New Year's, and she'll tell you, she's never felt better in her life.*

He's right. I stopped drinking soda and immediately felt more energy. Even diet soda made me feel weird. Maybe it was the caffeine? Anthony said something about soda depleting magnesium? I don't know. What I do know is that my brain cleared, like a thick fog lifted and all my cravings for anything sweet were gone.

Eating Out

If you do cook every single meal in your own kitchen, good on you. But, forgive me for saying, you should really get out more. Having fun is just as essential to good health as fruits and vegetables.

When reading a menu, watch out for these words: fried, sautéed, smothered, caramelized. If a dish has cream in it, avoid it. Once, I was off dairy for a long time, and then I went to my favorite Italian place and said, "I'm going to indulge tonight." I got penne à la vodka. The sauce is more cream than vodka. I slurped it down, burped politely into my napkin, and felt disgusting and bloated—but satisfied. Jionni had to roll me to the car later. In the middle of the night, I got sharp pains in my gut. Like an alien was stabbing me with knife. They weren't as bad as pregnancy contractions, but these cramps was the closest I've experienced. I'm telling you, this was agony! I writhed on the bed for hours with this, and literally thought my bowels were rotting inside me.

In the morning, I called my doctor and said, "I'm going to die."

"You're not going to die," he said. "You have gas."

He told me that I'd been eating healthy for so long, my pancreas (some gland or organ) that is responsible for breaking down dairy and fat in my guts couldn't handle the overload, and it freaked out. I'd basically transformed my body into being incapable of digesting fattening food! Anyway, moral to the story: when you think you're going to have a great time and pig out on something decadent, your body might torture you, and then, after putting you through hell, you are rewarded with explosive diarrhea. The End. Great story, right?

For that reason alone, I try to eat right when I'm going out. You don't have any control over what's served to you in a restaurant. The description might sound healthy, but the cook is probably adding sugar and butter to make it taste better so you keep coming back. So hedge your bets and order what the chef can't mess with.

- **Italian.** Even at a pasta place, there are always a few salad options and a piece of grilled chicken or fish with broccoli rabe. Yum.
- **Japanese.** Sushi is usually safe no matter what you order, but if possible, substitute brown rice for white.
- **Chinese.** A toughie, because everything is usually smothered in some sugary sauce or fried. The best you can do here is steamed veggies and shrimp with a little drizzle of soy sauce. Take the fortune, leave the cookie.
- **Mexican.** Get your fajita bowl at Chipotle with chicken, brown rice, black beans, tomatoes, lettuce, salsa, no cheese, no sour cream, yes guacamole.

Takeout

From a desk lunch to an ordered dinner, always go for the three S's:

- **Salad.** There are so many Just Salads– or Sweetgreens–type places around these days. It really has been a huge shift in fast food and we should all be grateful we can go into the corner lunch place and get a beautiful chopped salad with a huge combination of veggies and protein sources. I mean, kale is as common as regular lettuce. If you don't have a salad place near you, you can always order a salad at Wendy's or the deli.

- **Soup.** It can be kind of awkward to order a soup for lunch and take it to the park to eat. You need a flat surface for the bowl, and a spoon. So much easier to get a big sandwich that you can eat with one hand while you push your kid on the swing. BUT—if you can deal with it, soup is full of veggies and vitamins that have been boiled together, just waiting to get into your body and flood you with nutrients. It's filling because of the liquid, so you feel full on fewer calories.

- **Sandwich—hold the bread.** You don't want to get a big hero with a loaf of bread. But a wrap sandwich is a decent option for lunch or a quick meal. What I do is take it apart, and rewrap it with half the tortilla. They always overwrap those things. It's like double wrapping your Christmas presents. Why? It's a waste. If possible, get a sandwich that is wrapped in lettuce leaves. It might not be on the menu, but just ask for it and see what happens.

At the Bar

Even if you're in the mood to be bad, you can still be good to your body. I have only three drinks these days:

- **Vodka seltzer.** It keeps you hydrated sugar-free with no-carb vodka, so it's only a hundred calories per glass.
- **Red wine.** I love my Merlot and Pinot so much, I built a wine cellar in my house. I used to live in the basement. Now, my bottles do, and they have cute, safe little nooks to sleep in until I go down there and pillage.
- **Champagne.** On special occasions, there's nothing like popping a cork. But beware: Champagne is secretly sweet and full of sugar. If you don't take in a lot of sweet stuff, drinking bubbly will give you a pounding headache the next day. I have a glass to celebrate, and then move back to Pinot.

Some of my old favorite cocktails are probably why I got so chubby on *Jersey Shore*. Nowadays, I don't touch:

- **Sugar drinks**. Rum and Coke? Forget it! Anything with Kahlúa or Baileys is like a candy bar in a glass. Even drinks that taste sour are full of sugar, like margaritas or vodka tonics. The sweeter the drink, the higher the Hangover Index.

• **Beer.** Liquid bread. Nothing tastes better on a hot day by the pool, but one beer is the carb equivalent of half a bagel. You can't down a six pack of light beer, and fit into your shorts the next day. So don't even try.

CHAPTER FIVE

Strong Sense of Self

"**D**o the world a favor. Kill yourself and your whole family."

"Get off my TV, you fat ugly bitch. I need to shower five times just looking at you."

"When Snooki gives birth, the baby will walk right out of her vagina."

These lines were things people have written about me on Twitter and other sites. Social media is ground zero for bullies. Anyone can say anything. Losers become warriors behind a keyboard (especially when anonymous). I despise viciousness on the Internet. I wish those rude assholes would just go in a corner, play with themselves, and leave innocent people alone.

It's not a secret that I'm not the most liked person on the planet. You can't please all the people most of the time. But some people *really* don't like me. They say I'm an abomination to society, that I should be killed. Really? Killed? For partying too hard when I was young? Seems a bit extreme. The haters write their savage tweets because they are insecure, unhappy in their own lives, and jealous of other people's successes. I know a lot of people hate me because I got famous off of partying. I would hate me, too. Like, *Bitch you are rich and famous because you like to drink. Why couldn't that be me?* I just got lucky. I don't get why my luck takes away from a complete stranger's happiness, though.

So what do I do when someone on Twitter says, "You lost weight, but you're still a dumb slut?" (Damn, I hope Jionni doesn't find out.) My strategy is, first, to remind myself that these assholes don't know me. If they ever met me and hung out with me for five minutes, they would change their minds. Whatever their idea of me is, I happen to be a cool person. I know who I am and what I do all day. I'm a great mother, a loving fiancée, and a good friend. In our society, everyone judges one another and everyone has an opinion that's usually based on lies or half-truths. So I judge their opinions of me with emotional detachment. When people tweet that I'm a fat loser who should be shot, I know it's obnoxious, jealousy-based, and just plain wrong. Especially the fat part. They get to say what they think, and I get to say, "Bitch, please, you have no idea what you're talking about."

I refuse to let anyone bring me down with nonsense. So if you're having issues with bullying or have to deal with out-of-line haters, know that their attention is confirmation of only one thing: they are awful and disgusting. If they are taking the time out of their life to trash you publicly, they care enough about you to try to bring you down. It's sad that there will always be rude, ignorant, and judgmental people. But it's up to you to say, "Screw them, I'm fabulous." Stick together, send out positive vibes, and stand up against bullying and jerkoffs. Hair-flip them all day. Better yet, kill them with kindness.

I reply to haters every day. It's how I flex my inner strength. I retweet the mean ones, and turn it into a joke or try to be funny about it. You stand up to trolls and haters by not taking them seriously. These are not serious people. If they were, they'd be too busy with their own lives to trash me on Twitter. I shine a light on that, and take the power back.

My attitude might seem super strong, but I've been dealing with bullies for a long, long time, starting when I was a kid. I handle them so well now because I've had a lot of practice.

Mean Girls

My earliest hater experiences took place where most of us lose our bullying virginity: high school.

HERE'S STEPHANIE

When Nicole and I were in high school, we got bullied pretty bad. There were these older girls, seniors when we were freshman, who despised us. To this day, I have no idea what they hated so much about us. They came after our whole group of friends, but picked on Nicole and me the most. How did they torment us? They wore T-shirts that said mean things about us, prank-called us at 2:00 a.m., egged our houses, spread viscous rumors about us, nothing I'd care to divulge, but really cruel, horrible stuff. Every day, I left the school in tears. We were fifteen years old, and they were eighteen. They tortured us every day, relentlessly. This was way before Facebook. I can only imagine what they would have done now. Things were different back then, too. Bullying isn't tolerated anymore. If they had tried to do it today, they would have all been expelled.

High school for me was like *Orange Is the New Black*. You're stuck there. Even if you're sweet and innocent, you can't ignore it when scary, dangerous people have it out for you. The seniors always bullied me and my girls. We were cute and pretty, the cheerleaders. In hindsight, I can see how we might've been a little full of ourselves. But we didn't do anyone harm and were just having a good time.

One day they came to school with shirts on and each one had our name and mean things about us written on the shirts. They would call me slut and whore and say I took in the ass, which I never did in high school. Then the last day of school, the girls brought a video camera and asked us if we had any last words for them. Basically saying, "Bye, slut, before we smoke you." They were awful. We were so glad and relieved when they graduated, but then the next year's senior girls bullied us, too. I wasn't going to have another year of getting tortured and that's when I stood up for myself.

HERE'S STEPHANIE

Nicole let most of it roll off her back like water. But she had her limits. There was one time when all of them were wearing the T-shirts they made about us, calling us trash, sluts, etc. Nicole, who was even smaller then than she is now, walked right up to the main girl, stood on her tiptoes and screamed, "You wanna wear a shirt about me? I'll rip it off your back!" We'd been dealing with them for months already, and Nicole just had enough. She got right up in her face, and went crazy. It didn't stop them, but I felt a lot better about it. Another time, Nicole kicked in the door of one of their trucks. Again, tiny Nicole, kicking a car. When the girl confronted her about

> *it, she said, "Yeah, I kicked your truck, and I'll do it again!"*
> *We all cowered in fear behind Nicole, and she took these*
> *bullies to task.*

A Sore Thing

During the *Jersey Shore* years, aka "the dawn of social media," the hate rained down on me like a hurricane. Twitter was only a couple of years old by then, and from the very beginning, people used it as a way to anonymously insult celebrities. I didn't think of myself as a celebrity—still don't. I know it sounds schizo, but my TV persona, Snooki, was only one part of who I was/am. It was the only part people knew, so they assumed that the horny, drunk, sloppy girl was all of me. They resented the fact that I got famous from being a drunken idiot on the beach, and, as I said before, I completely understand. Anyone can be a drunken idiot on the beach, but I was the one who got famous for it.

It takes more than just jealousy of someone else's success to turn a normal, ordinary citizen into a cruel, destructive, sexist pig when he's anonymous behind a keyboard. There has to be something missing in a person who takes time in his day to attack strangers using a pseudonym. How unhappy do you have to be to take that route? How hollow inside? I have no idea. But this pattern of behavior is only getting worse. It's part of the culture now, and despicable as it is, anyone who's in the public eye has to deal with it.

I know a lot of celebrities and regular people go after their haters, and get in Twitter Wars over the stupidest shit. That's way too much drama for this mama. No judgments at all about how others handle it. We all manage our lives as we see fit. A lot of people get off on confrontation. It brings excitement into their lives. I have friends that love drama. They are addicted to it. They complain about someone doing them wrong, but once they don't have the drama, they get bored with their lives. I watch them struggle with the asshole boyfriend and the bad boss, and they keep going back for more. I don't think they can change. Drama addiction is something that you're born with, or you pick up at some point and can't let go of. It's just who they are, like pathological liars. They know they do it. They know it's wrong. But they do it anyway. It's just how they're built.

Well, that's not how I am at all. I'd rather never get in a fight again. I just want to skip around and be happy. I don't have time for drama, or the inclination to cause it or keep it going. I *never* pick fights on social media, or in real life. *Jersey Shore* was full of drama—hardly any of it mine—because it was a TV show. We were drunk. When some people are drunk, they like to fight and they turn nasty. If you look at the old shows, you'll see: I avoided fighting. I just wanted a boyfriend.

But people associate the show with fighting, and they associate the show with me. Therefore, they think I like to fight. It couldn't be more wrong. Instead of ignoring the haters or confronting them, I set out to prove them wrong about me and return their fire with kindness and humor.

I had a great opportunity to do just that on a TV show called *H8R*. Mario Lopez was the host, and he invited me to be on the first episode, because I guess I had more haters than anyone else. For a while there, I was the most hated celebrity in America, in particular, the Italian American community. Mario found this one guy named Nick who despised me. The show filmed him doing a rant about me, saying I was a drunk donkey, that I stank like a sausage factory in Newark, and should go slither back under the slime-covered rock from whence I came or just go shoot myself in the face.

You know, a typical Wednesday for me.

Nick hated me for making money on TV and took it as a personal insult that I made more in an episode than his cop father did in a year. Immediately, I thought, *Why isn't he so angry that cops don't get the salary they deserve?* We should all be furious about that! My salary on *Jersey Shore* had nothing to do with his father's income. It's like saying, "Sushi is expensive. Therefore, I hate tomatoes." Makes no sense.

Clearly this guy was taking out his anger and hostility at the world on me. Fame turns anyone into a target for other people's unhappiness. You become this figure that people can point at, get mad at, and say horrible things about because it's like you're not a real person in real life.

Mario arranged an ambush. This guy Nick was hanging out at some bar in L.A., just chilling, shooting pool. I walked in with light-up stiletto booties that were so freakin' cute and did my hair nice and had on a sweet black skirt suit. I thought my outfit would soften Nick's cold-dead heart. I went right up to him and told him I saw the video he made about me.

He said, "She speaks English. She's not drunk."

I guess he didn't like my outfit.

One of the things I get most annoyed with is how people will say anything on Twitter and Instagram, but if they met me face-to-face, they would never be so rude. Nick didn't have that problem. He went on and on, insulting me, saying I was a stupid slob, that I lied about being Italian (I have never, ever, claimed to be Italian; I was adopted by an Italian American family) and that my new novel *A Shore Thing* sucked.

"Did you read it?" I asked. Of course, he didn't. "If you read my book, you'd know it's really good."

He was judging my book, and me, by the cover, which I also didn't get. The cover of *A Shore Thing* is awesome. I looked really pretty that day. My parents taught me early on that if you judge people for their appearance alone, you're shallow. If you're cruel and mean about it, you're a bully.

I would have just walked out then and there, but it was for Mario's show and I had to see it through. I asked Nick if I could cook him and his family dinner. If we hung out and broke bread, he'd realize that he was hating on a sweetheart. He could have refused, but he didn't. The dinner idea could still go wrong if his family was as rude and obnoxious as he was. I'd be alone against a mob of haters, one of them a cop with a gun.

First, Nick and I went to a supermarket to buy ingredients. I've always believed this: when you're shopping for food or anything, you get in a better mood. On the way there, I mentioned that we had something in common, that his dad was a cop, and mine was a firefighter. Nick said, "I didn't know that."

Exactly my point! He didn't know *anything* about me. You know that saying, "When you assume, you're an asshole," (or something like that). I told him that out of respect for my father, one of the charities I donated time and money to was burn victims. That changed his perspective of me a little. You could see a light go on, like he was thinking, *What? She donates to charity? She didn't spend all her money on light-up booties?* He clued in, that maybe I was a bit more than the Smurf he watched on TV.

Nick treated me a little nicer at the store. I tried to joke around with him to loosen him up and asked, "What if I poison your family?" Maybe that wasn't a good joke to open with. He looked genuinely afraid.

At one point, he put two coconuts against his chest, jiggled them around and said, "Look at me, I'm on *Jersey Shore.*"

I said, "You don't need those. You've got boobs already." Later, I fed him a pickle from the jar and told him, "You have to suck on it," which was supposed to be funny. He smiled, showing a tiny glimmer of a sense of humor. If you spend ten minutes with someone, they're either less or more annoying than you thought. But at least you have something real to base your opinion on. If he still hated me after hanging out with me, okay. My problem with him was that he hated me without ever looking into my eyes or talking to me.

We drove straight to his parents' house. I hoped they weren't expecting a gourmet feast, because they'd hate me even more when they tasted my cooking. As soon as I walked in the door, his family looked at me like I was an alien. There were half a dozen people, all staring at me. They commented on my blinking shoes. One guy said, "Are you signaling a turn with those?" which was actually pretty funny. If I weren't feeling so awkward, I would have laughed.

I introduced myself to every one of them, shaking their hands and looking them in the eye. "Me and my mom make chicken cutlets on Sunday, so that's what I'm going to make tonight," I said.

I swear, they looked shocked, like, *Snooki has a mother? They cook together? But that's so normal.*

Also normal: having a glass of wine while you cook. That's *my* normal, anyway. So we did. I pulled Nick's mom aside to get to know her better. She smiled at me, but talked trash about the show. The usual stuff, how I'm a bad example to young girls and how I misrepresent Italians. She also didn't like how I showed my boobs and butt on the show.

"When you were twenty-one, you never went to a bar and had a good time?" I asked.

"No," she said. I'm like, *Bullshit!* But, as a polite, respectful guest in her home, I didn't dare question it.

Nick's dad was a lot nicer right off the bat. He said, as a cop, he sees a lot of "Snooki personalities," meaning party girls, on the street. I'd been recently arrested for being a "Snooki personality" when I got drunk and disorderly on the beach in Seaside Heights.

"It was embarrassing when that happened," I said. "I made a mistake, we all do. It changed my mind about life, that maybe I need to calm down with partying." It was sort of like talking to my own dad.

He asked about my nickname. I said, "My real name is Nicole and I'd like it if you called me that."

"Your name is Nicole?"

They were all surprised. They didn't even know my name, but they thought they knew exactly who and what I was.

By night's end, they seemed to like me. I didn't burn the chicken, set the house on fire, go crazy, or dance on the table. We had a glass or two of wine, and I was my charming, sweet self. Not The Snooki (as I think of my on-camera persona). I was just Nicole. Love me, hate me, and anywhere in between. But don't make your choice until you get to know me a little. I made my point and left feeling pretty good about it.

Anyway, *H8R* wasn't a hit. I think maybe ten people saw the episode, and they were probably all members of Nick's family.

The Governor of New Jersey Tried to Eat Me

Even when I'm trying to help others, I take it on the chin. Governor Chris Christie and I once went toe-to-toe on the boardwalk in Seaside Heights at a Hurricane Sandy fund-raiser.

He'd previously trashed *Jersey Shore*, saying the cast and the show were bad for New Jersey. He tried to make it harder for the show to film in Seaside Heights, and *a lot* more expensive. But his attempt to censor us didn't work. We kept on rolling for another three years. Personally, I think Christie does a much worse job representing New Jersey than we did. We were just a bunch of drunk kids having a great time at the beach. But the governor has been beyond rude to me and so many other people, telling reporters to "sit down and shut up," yelling at teachers on the boardwalk. And then there's was the whole Bridgegate thing. (Some of my tweets about that were picked up by legit news services, which cracked me up. It was sort of like when John McCain and I got to be friends. It's all just so weird, and surreal, that politicians and I have anything to do with each other!)

Anyway, when Christie and I finally met at the Hurricane Sandy event, I introduced myself and said, "I hope you can start to like us." Then he leaned in close and told me why he doesn't. His expression was full of hate. I was in Seaside Heights that day to raise money for victims, and he's taking time out of his governor day to insult me to my face? Deena, a castmate, tried to distract him, but he said, "I'm talking to her." It was so obnoxious! He outweighs me by a thousand pounds, and he leaned really low and got up in my face, trying to scare me. I didn't back down, though. I said, "Why are you standing so close?"

I was definitely intimidated; Christie is a scary man. I wish the cameras picked up everything he said to me because he was beyond rude. When the conversation ended, I walked away. My knees were shaking. There's nothing I could have said to Christie about my love of New Jersey or my commitment to gay rights and teachers' rights that would have changed his opinion about me. Still, I tried to be polite and respectful, no matter what. Rudeness doesn't go far, although Christie is trying to take it all the way to the White House. We'll see how that works out for him. But that's all I'll say about that.

I love this quote I came across one day on Instagram: "You don't need to take revenge. Just sit back and wait because Karma will get hold of those that hurt you and if you are lucky, God will let you watch."

Supernatural Disgust

Last year, I was asked to appear on the TV show *Supernatural*. I was a huge fan of the show for a while. The actors had, in the past, made jokes on and off camera about seeing demon Snookis in dark corners, so the producers got the bright idea of having me do a cameo as an actual demon. I nearly wet my pants; I was so excited. It'd always been a dream of mine, since I was just a little girl, to be a demon. I also dreamed of being a bride. A demon bride would be the ultimate ultimate ultimate.

Supernatural wasn't my first cameo or scripted acting job. I'd done skits as myself on *Jimmy Kimmel Live!* and was in *The Three Stooges* movie (and got my eyes poked by a Stooge; another dream come true). This part was playing myself again, but as if I weren't a human, but an evil spirit living inside a meat suit that looked exactly like me. My scene, beginning to end, was about four minutes or Demon Snooki talking to the Winchester brothers about some other another satanic being they were trying to track down. The best part: As a demon, they'd CGI me with glowing red eyes—which I would rock hard.

I told Jionni, "I'm gonna be a demon!"

He asked, "What are you now?"

See what I mean, how he annoys the shit out of me?

So Mom and I went to Canada for the shoot. I felt queasy on the flight, and all day. I remember telling my mom how nauseous and tired I was. We thought it was because I was traveling so much. Soon after, I found out I was around two months pregnant with Giovanna when I was there. My daughter was a little eggy when I played a demon. No wonder she ended up giving me nightmares.

In case you weren't aware, Canada is freeezzzing. The entire daylong shoot was cold as fuck, but also beyond fun. Memorizing the lines didn't come naturally to me, because my memory is for shit. We worked it out that someone fed me the line, and then I put the Snooki mojo on it. I was used to reality, which means you just say whatever you're thinking. Scripted was a different experience for me, and I really got into it. The two male leads—actors Jared Padalecki and Jensen Ackles—were generous and patient with me. I didn't realize how tall they were until I posed for a picture next to them. They were both a foot taller than me. It made me feel like the smallest demon from hell, even in my blood-red, six-inch heels.

Naturally, I posted photos with the Winchesters and tweeted how much fun I had on set. It was all such a positive, awesome experience. The cast and crew on *Supernatural* made me feel more like a princess than a demon. A big thank-you to everyone involved!

As soon as that photo of me with Jared and Jenson went up, the geek hate came rolling down the Twittersphere like an avalanche. I was taken by surprise about it (you think I'd learn). The fact that I was a fan of the show didn't stop the fanniacs from treating it like the second coming of the anti-Christ, saying I would ruin the entire series and would destroy their love of the show, that I'd suck (of course), and other nasty stuff. I didn't let it get to me. But, jeez, the amount of bile spewn could have filled a swimming pool. It's like I went to their houses and shat on their beds. I was like, *Dudes, you gotta relax.*

It helped that, for each mean tweet, there were twenty replies, telling the hater to shut the fuck up. My lovies and boo boos rushed to defend me. It was so cool. I felt a little like Beyoncé. If someone dares to insult Queen Bey online, the Bey-hive swarms in for the kill. I want to thank my fans for having my back and telling my haters to take their loser asses somewhere else.

When the show aired, my cameo turned out great. I looked hot in a red dress, and delivered my lines like a pro. Once the fans saw it, they thought it was hysterical and actually enjoyed it. The whole avalanche of hate was for nothing.

People are idiots.

The Straw that Broke the Camera's Back

My usual strategy with online trolls is to return fire with sugar. I reply to their tweet in a funny, nice way, and more often than not, they say, "You're actually cool, and I'm an asshole." I completely agree. I never say, *Oh, fuck you.* If I did that, I'd be feeding into the trolls. You just can't do that and expect to live on social media.

I can take criticism about pretty much anything. My appearance.

My brands. My shows. But when people write terrible things about my kids, I draw the line. I posted photos of my son and daughter on Instagram because I'm proud of them and wanted to show off my beautiful babies. My fans asked to see the pix, so I put them up gladly. Ninety-nine percent of the comments were kind and supportive. It's a heady rush, when thousands of people tell you exactly what you believe in your heart, that your babies are the cutest, sweetest little nuggets on Earth.

And then there was the 1 percent of assholes who wrote horrible, disgusting things about my children, including perverted sexual comments. It's hard to believe that some people are so miserable that they'd denegrate a stranger's children to feel better about themselves. What kind of sicko does that? I would never belittle someone to make me feel better about myself, let alone write things about innocent, harmless babies.

Talking smack about my family felt like an attack, like someone was trying to do my loved ones physical harm. When I read that shit, my heart started racing, and my adrenaline pumped through my veins. If the hater had been sitting in the same room as me, I would have killed the bitch. It was simply impossible to reply to that kind of fire with sugar. I felt I couldn't ignore it, either. It was too personal, and upsetting. My kids are my life. I'm a mama leopard, I will always rush in to defend them.

So, the only possible solution was a drastic one. Although I loved sharing my kids' pictures, I had to stop doing it. It came down to my personal comfort level and being protective of my family. If I'm in a public space, like a playground, and a stranger lurking by the swings gives me a bad feeling, I'd call the cops and leave that place. Instagram, Twitter, and Facebook are just like the playground, and I'm making sure to protect my kids from pervs and psychokillers who might be lurking around.

I'm not denying the free speech of douchebags to say disgusting things online. What makes our nation great is anyone's right to be as hateful as he wants, to speak from the cold, black hollow where his heart should be. But I don't have to put up with comments that piss me off, either. So I don't post photos of my children anymore. It saves me the aggravation. I've learned the hard way that if you know something you do is guaranteed to cause you pain and aggravation, then stop doing it. Life is short, and so am I. I don't have time to stress myself out. Simple math.

HERE'S MOM

When I see what some people say about Nicole, it's hard. It's really hard. I'm not going to sugar coat it and say it rolls off my back. Someone is insulting my daughter and my grandchildren. It brings out your protective nature. But what can I do? Drive to someone's house? Write angry comments back? That's not my style, and I've always tried to encourage

Nicole to take the high road. So that's what I do. I take the high road myself—and I have a big glass of red wine every night.

I haven't always been as calm about Nicole having a public life. During the first season of Jersey Shore, there was a night early on when she called home and said she wasn't making friends and wanted to leave the show. My first reaction: come home. I knew she was going to be in such a party mode when she went there. It was a real possibility that she'd crash and burn. Her father encouraged her to stay, which was the right thing to do, but my instinct was to get her the hell out of there. In hindsight, she's gotten where she is today because she stuck it out. But as a mother, I was a nervous wreck about her staying. And then when the show aired, I was a wreck about how Nicole would be perceived.

Occasionally, people in my community gave me funny looks about Jersey Shore. I'm sure they were all talking about it. A few actually asked me how I could let Nicole act like that on TV. But most of the time, people didn't approach me because they knew I would break down. They didn't want to upset me. It was upsetting! Of course it was. Everyone was pointing to her and saying she represented everything bad about our country. It hurt to hear that.

But it worked out fine in the end. Now she's happy and successful, married to a wonderful man, caring for two *perfect babies and living in a beautiful home. I don't care what anyone says about Nicole. It's all good. We are blessed.*

My mom knows me. She has known me since I was six months old. People online don't know me. I've taken a lot of shit for saying, "I'm a good person" in my own defense, in particular, on the day back in 2010 when I got arrested on the beach for public intoxication and kept repeating that phrase to the cops as they put me in handcuffs and dragged me into a squad car. I knew then, as I know now, that I *am* a good person. How am I so sure?

I love my family.

I try to bring joy and laughs into the world.

If a friend is upset, I'd do anything to make her happy again.

I support a dozen charities with my money and time.

I wouldn't hurt a fly.

I don't steal, do drugs, lie, or cheat.

I work hard to give my kids a good life.

No one can change these basic facts. Whether thousands of strangers—or just a few obnoxious jerkoffs at school or at work—try to define you, your best defense is a strong sense of self. You have to know who you are, remind yourself who you are, and make a list of all your awesome qualities to combat the negativity that comes from jealousy, resentment, insecurity, and drama addiction. If you ever feel taken down by hate, just love yourself right back up.

CHAPTER SIX

Strong Family

We all need someone in our lives that has the balls to say to our face, "What the fuck is *wrong* with you? You're acting like a friggin' moron! Jesus Christ, asshole. Get your shit together!"

In my life, that's what family is for.

I don't have just one family. I've got a bunch of different branches.

The Family I Was Born To

As I have made crystal clear, I know who I am. But, because I was adopted, I didn't always know *what* I was.

I'm color blind and have no prejudice about any race or religion. It's a big world, full of people and ideas. There is room for everyone, and we all bring new, cool things to the table. That's my attitude about it. My adoptive parents are Italian American, and I was only too happy and comfortable to include myself in that culture. It was all I knew. I was adopted, and I adapted to be like my parents. I was like a dog raised by sheep that thinks it's a sheep. Surely you've seen the videos on YouTube. Or like a hippo that thinks it's a giraffe. That's me. An Italian American hippo.

Growing up, I didn't question it, or care about my real cultural heritage or ethnicity. I loved my parents. I loved our way of doing things. I didn't need answers since I didn't have any concerns. It felt like an insult to them to delve deeper in the details of the adoption. In the past, when I casually asked Mom about my biological parents, she would get upset and didn't want to talk about them. Jionni pushed it when I was pregnant, and Mom assured him that my biological parents were healthy and that there was no cause for concern. Even if she told him, "Her parents were crack-smoking midgets with leprosy," it's not like that information would change anything. The entire discussion seemed irrelevant.

When Lorenzo was born, he became the first person I'd ever met who shared my blood. Pause to take that in. It took me a long time to fully absorb what that meant to me. I bonded with my parents as closely as any child—adopted or biological—possibly could. But my parents weren't my blood. Jionni wasn't my blood, either (thank God, because if he were, we'd be incesting). I love my parents and husband as deeply as a daughter and wife can. But until Lorenzo, I couldn't look at the faces of my family and see myself. Lorenzo resembles me. He came out of me, was made inside me. Half of his DNA came from me.

So that got me thinking about what I was. I was born in Chile. But I wasn't sure that made me of Chilean descent. I sort of looked South American, but was I really? I didn't have a clue. I started to wonder what tribe we came from. Not the specific family. Honestly, I have no desire or need to come face-to-face with my birth parents. But I was starting to get curious about what culture I came from, and what part of the world. If Lorenzo were ever asked in school to point at a map and say where his ancestors came from, I wanted him to be able to answer that question from his daddy's side and his mommy's. Daddy's ancestors are from Italy. Saying his mom's people come from Marlboro, New York, didn't seem to cut it.

So, one afternoon, Lorenzo and I went to a genetic testing lab in north Jersey. Paparazzi were stalking me then, and they wrote the stupidest shit about my visit there, saying I took my son to do a paternity test, as if I didn't know who the father of my child was. Like I forgot who I was having sex with for the last three years. Does a person forget that? Argh. Anyway, I met with a genetics counselor, a nice, patient woman who told me how the whole thing worked, the way the DNA testing was done, what I could learn. Ninety-nine percent of it whistled through my ears, but I got the essentials. By sticking a Q-tip in my mouth and swiping the inside of my cheek— like a pap smear of my mouth—she'd get a sample of my saliva, which contained enough of my DNA to squirt into a computer that would analyze it and spit back out my ethnicity.

A couple of weeks later, I went back to the lab for the results. I figured I was mainly South American going by the clues I had: my parents adopted me from Santiago, Chile, and my skin is naturally tan. Then again, I could be from a galaxy far, far away.

I told the genetics counselor, "If I'm an alien, that would be the best-case scenario, because I've always wanted to be an alien."

I didn't mean like an alien citizen, like someone from another country who lived here illegally. I meant little greenies from outer space. I could be originally from another galaxy, and stuck here on Earth, like E.T. I've always felt like I was from another planet. I wondered if their computer had alien DNA in its files.

The counselor laughed, thinking. I was kidding. I said, "I'm serious."

"Well, you're human," she said.

Disappointingly, I'm a normal, red-blooded Earthling. And what part of the Earth do my people come from? All over it, actually. My DNA results were all over the map. Here's the complete list of my people:

Romani
Indian (as in Bollywood)
South Asian

East Asian

Middle Eastern

Jewish

Croatian

Macedonian

Slovakian

Russian

Spanish

Hundreds of years ago, if not thousands, my ancestors probably started fornicating with each other in India or Thailand, and then they migrated northwest, screwing their way through Persia and Israel. More interracial fucking in Eastern Europe, and then they landed in southern Europe, continuing to have unprotected sex all over that continent, before migrating south to Chile, where they gave birth to me.

I was really excited about being Romani, aka a gypsy. Gypsies are cool. They have great fashion, can tell the future, and they're outrageous. This might be the part of me that felt like I was from another planet. Sometimes, I feel psychic and can predict things. Being part gypsy explains that. I've *always* liked head scarfs and dangly earrings. It all made sense!

I'm also Asian. I had no idea. I'm way into that. Asians are hot.

The Jewish part threw me. I was raised strictly Catholic and am a true believer in God and Jesus. I don't go to church as much as I should, but I strongly identify myself as Catholic. Hearing that I was part Jewish confused me.

When Jionni saw that on the list, he teased me about it. "You celebrate Yom Kippur?"

I said, "Jewish is, like, a part of Europe."

This comment aired on *Snooki & Jwoww.* I got a lot of shit for it on Twitter. It's not entirely wrong, by the way. Some Jewish ethnic groups do come from Europe. I looked it up. So all the people who railed at me about that line can SUCK IT. You can have Jewish blood and not practice the Jewish religion. In fact, that's the case for most of the Jews I know. I thought Jewish was *just* a religion. I didn't know that it was also a race, like white, black, or brown. Now I know, and I am with you, Jews! We are one.

I'm with all of you. Gypsies, Indians, Persians, and Slovakians. I've got a little bit of all these people inside me, and it's not crowded in here at all. I've always felt like the cutest babies and most gorgeous people are mixed race. A little of this, a little of that. It's sexy to be a mutt. As it turns out, that's what I am. I can't point to any one place, or any one culture, and say, "That's me." I can spin the entire globe and claim a connection to just about anywhere my finger lands on it.

Lorenzo is from everywhere, too, with a particularly strong connection on his daddy's side to Italy. Finding out what we are was baffling at first. It challenged the idea of myself I always had.

But coming from dozens of different places didn't really change where I was coming from, if you get my meaning. I'm still me. I already knew who I was, and that didn't change.

My blood had been wandering the world in search of a home for generations. But I have a home, a family, a religion, and a strong sense of who I am and where I fit in. What I am didn't really matter that much after all.

The Family That Chose Me

My parents, Helen and Andy, always told me that they chose me, that I was special and they could see it from first sight. The idea that I was special, at least in their eyes, stuck with me.

HERE'S MOM

We adopted Nicole when she was six months old. Andy and I were just thrilled to finally have a baby. We didn't consciously think, We're going to raise her to be a hard-working and responsible person. We just set out to raise a happy, healthy child, and to give someone love and get some love in return. Nicole's core values—that you should be close and respectful to your parents and that family is everything—come from what she observed growing up at home and in the homes of her friends.

My marriage with Nicole's father dissolved when Nicole

was thirteen. She always says the divorce didn't affect her. In the beginning it probably did, when we first told her we were going to separate. But in the end, she realized that it was the best for all of us. I believe that being the child of divorce can strengthen the bonds of marriage for the next generation because you see how things can go wrong and what you don't want in a relationship. I just love Jionni to death and I look at their marriage as very strong and solid. They're of the same mind-set in terms of how to raise their kids, how to live, where to live, what they want for their family. Their personalities are different enough to keep the relationship interesting.

Nicole had the large extended family of her close friends, and we all lived in close proximity to each other. We celebrated Christmas, Thanksgiving, and Easter together. It adds fun, value, and depth to everything when you share it with a lot of other people. I don't come from a large family, and neither does Andy. So our friendships gave her the large family experience even though she was the single child of divorced parents. I'm sure one of the reasons she was so attracted to Jionni was his coming from a big, close family that she could see herself become a part of.

Our family was always small, and it kept getting smaller. My dad had two brothers who died of cancer when I was young. My dad's parents died, too. My mom had two brothers, too. One lives far away and I don't really talk to him. But one, Ben, and I were really close. He was Mom's best friend and he came over a lot to do yardwork at the house. He was a cool uncle, and we talked about smoking weed and drinking. When I was seventeen, he died suddenly of a brain aneurysm. It was so heartbreaking to lose him like that. It's not like he was sick for a while and we had a chance to get ready for it or had an idea it was going to happen. He was hanging around, raking leaves. And then we found out he was gone. It was a huge loss for Mom and me. I miss him still, but I think his ghost checks in to say hello sometimes.

As an only child, I got a lot of attention, and was spoiled, which I loved. But I also missed having that big extended family of aunts and uncles. More important, I always wished I had sisters and brothers to play with in the house. I begged my parents to adopt another kid, but it never happened. And then my parents got divorced. The split didn't scar me for life or drive me into therapy. I was sad when it happened, but it didn't damage my soul, or make me think love was a sham. Nothing like that. I know people who were deeply affected by their parents' divorce, but that seemed to happen in ugly, hateful situations when the exes were fighting each other over who got to keep the silverware. Well, my parents didn't give a shit about silverware, and neither do I. They didn't go to war over a fork and kept their emotions under control.

But no one ends a marriage being best friends. As a family, we went through some bumpy times, and it wasn't fun. Dad moved out and got his own place. For half the time, it was just Mom and me. The other half, it was Dad and me. Love my parents to death, but my home life at both their houses was kind of lonely. When I dreamed about my future, I always pictured myself in a sexy-yet-stable marriage with a lot of kids, something different from what I grew up with. Not saying my childhood sucked! I grew up great, and was lucky to be adopted into an awesome family. It just didn't work out for my parents in their marriage. I wanted something different for my marriage, and for my kids.

My parents and I are very close. Mom comes to our house in New Jersey every week to spend the day with the kids. She works for Snooki Inc., my company that sells all my brands. My dad works on my finances. We're all in my career together. I want to provide for my parents like they did for me and, in our crazy world, that means I'm their boss. It can be hard to work with your family and sometimes we do have arguments. But they're the only people I really trust. I know they would never screw me over.

HERE'S JOEY

Helen and Andy are always around, helping Nicole out with the kids or with business. They're 100 percent supportive of her. Nicole has definitely given them reason to worry about

My mom used to be a nurse at an orthopedic practice. My dad bounced around at different jobs, but he was in the tire business and a volunteer firefighter. Being in business together for the last few years really changed the tone between my parents. In a bizarre way, like a family unit again. My parents get along great now. They've been divorced for thirteen years. So it took them ten years postdivorce to heal and get over it. Is that normal? Probably not. Nothing about our family is normal. Now that I'm a parent, I love and respect Mom and Dad even more because I know what goes into raising babies. Both my parents were at the hospital when I gave birth to both kids. I wouldn't have wanted it any other way.

If they couldn't stand the sight of each other, or if they got into a screaming match every time we were in the same room, it'd be awful. I've heard about that kind of situation and thank God that's not us. Every holiday would be a blood bath and a fight over who gets to see the babies. That would not work for me. I love Christmas too much to ruin it with drama. I'm one of those people who puts up their tree right after Halloween. The longer I can celebrate, the better. When I hear Christmas music, I'm instantly in a great mood. I love it all: drinking eggnog, buying gifts, wrapping presents, and how everyone on the street is smiling and people stop being Scrooges. When I was a kid, Christmases were always awesome. Mom and Dad spoiled me since I was the only kid in the house. They bought me dozens of presents. I'd wake up on Christmas morning and find a sea of wrapped boxes under the tree. I had to put on a good show of acting surprised as I opened each one. I found their hiding place when I was around nine, and snuck in there before the holiday to check on my prezzies, and drop heavy hints if I couldn't find the one thing I really wanted. It always turned up the next day.

This past Christmas, Giovanna's first, my first as a wife in our house, I hosted the holiday and asked that my parents stay overnight so they'd be here when Lorenzo woke up to find his presents under the tree. Mom and Dad were happy to do it. It warmed my heart, seeing them both—and Dad's fiancée, Laurie—with my kids on Christmas morning. I gave Mom and Dad a hard time when I was younger, and we fought over stupid shit like my partying too much. Now I understand where that was coming from. After I had Lorenzo, I realized how they felt about me, how worried they were. I know they're not worried about me anymore, and that makes me happy.

The Family I Chose

When Jionni and I got pregnant with Lorenzo, the three of us became the family I chose. Now we have Giovanna. Someday, we'll have a couple more babies. I built a house with five bedrooms. I'm determined to fill them up.

HERE'S JOEY

They're just a fun, loving pair. They seem like opposites—she's outgoing and he's quiet—but what they have in common, besides a sense of humor, are that they come from close families that share the same values. Jionni, as the youngest brother in his family, was the baby growing up. Now, he gets to be the head of his own family. His stepping up in this way is endearing to Nicole. It makes her feel protected and safe. I think Jionni filled the hero role for Nicole. He came into her life and saved her. He's given her stability, security, a person to pour all of her love and energy into. She's given him excitement, a family to call his own, adoration. The kids just seal the deal. Jionni and Nicole have a shared focus for the direction of their lives. Their family unit totally works.

No way in hell was I hiring a nanny. My son would not be raised by strangers. It's something I feel strongly about. It's not a judgment of anyone who hires a nanny. We all do what we have to do to make our lives work. Even when I was filming *Snooki & Jwoww,* we sorted things out so that Janice, Jionni's mom, and my mom took care of Lorenzo when Jionni and I couldn't.

I'm sure a nanny would do an excellent job of changing diapers, bottle feeding, and waving a stuffed animal in my son's face. But I didn't become a parent so I could hire someone else to wipe the crap off my son's balls. I wanted to do that myself! I had to experience every aspect of parenthood, from the shitty to the sublime, for my own selfish reasons, but also for Lorenzo's sake. It mattered to me that every person who cared for him was a member of his family. When he looked into the face of whoever was giving him a bath or feeding him or smiling at him, it would be someone he would know for the rest of his life. A nanny can be loving and genuinely caring for a child. But no matter how you slice it, he or she is being paid to do a job. It's just different. If not for the money, the nanny wouldn't be there. For me, that subtle distinction was enormous. Now that Lorenzo is older, I do have a regular babysitter to come in for a few hours now and then. But she's also a family friend who I've known for years, someone I trust completely. I do feel a little guilty about hiring any extra help. But, then again, I really need my sleep, especially with Giovanna still breastfeeding.

Oh God, my nipples! They're five inches long. I used a breast pump exclusively with Lorenzo because we had problems latching on. Giovanna knew exactly what she was doing right from the start, and latched on like a boss. Except for the birth, which wasn't fun, Giovanna has been an easy baby, mainly because we're smarter parents. We know what the fuck we're doing this time around. With Lorenzo, we were clueless about everything, super careful and watchful. With Giovanna, we're relaxed, and calmer, which benefits both kids.

When you have only one kid, you're laser-focused on everything he says and does. He becomes the little prince. As an only child, I totally took advantage of that. When the attention wasn't on me, I just didn't feel right so I'd do whatever I could to get it back: throw a tantrum, jump on the furniture, cry, crawl all over my parents. Lorenzo might've turned into a brat like I was if we hadn't given him a sister. When I think about how much attention Lorenzo got compared to Giovanna, I get pangs. Believe me, my daughter gets a lot of attention. But it pales in comparison to the little prince. She's a girl, though, and she'll learn how to get what she needs, and from who. I think it's telling that her first word was "Dada." See? She's smart. Giovanna knows I'm not going to let her get away with anything. Meanwhile, she's wrapping Jionni around her tiny, little fingers.

A friend once told me, "When you have one kid, the parents do a team defense. When you have two, it's one-on-one. When you have three or more, it's zone." I don't get most sports metaphors at all, but this one struck a nerve. Right now, Jionni is kind of in charge of Lorenzo and Giovanna is mine. After our third, what do we do? Jionni can take the downstairs, and I'll do upstairs? Or, even better, I'll cover my closet and bathroom. Jionni can handle the rest of the house.

Lorenzo is actually really independent. He can get his own juice and play with his toys by himself. So hopefully he can help us wrangle the future babies. He's going to be their big brother. Right now, he's not so into that job. He never talks to Giovanna. One day, I'm sure he'll love bossing her around. And she'll love annoying the shit out of him.

HERE'S STEPHANIE

I joke with Nicole and say, "You're a nicer person now that you have a family." She was always a sweetheart, but having kids grounded her. Her family is her support system, even though she's taking care of them. Just being a mom and having the purpose of raising kids gives her the strength to do just about anything.

My life is for my kids now. When I work, it's for them. I don't hustle to get myself a new bag or shoes. I hustle to pay for this house and my kids and their college. It's all about them. Having children gives my life depth and meaning. How I spend my days is important now. It's not about bullshit. It's about human beings.

I was pregnant two out of the last three summers. So this year, I'm going to take the summer off from pregnancy because I want to wear a bikini and feel good and drink a drink by the pool. I say that, and just watch. I'll probably get knocked up by accident again.

Whether it's the family you were born into, the family that chose you, or the family you choose, the closer you are, the stronger the ties, the stronger you are as an individual. If you have this whole army of people at your back, it's easy to be brave and launch yourself into the unknown. If you fall down, you know you have all these people to help you get back up on your feet.

To get the full family benefits, you have to be honest. If something is bothering you, you have to bring it up and get it out or you will just eventually blow up. Have the hard conversations. Work through your shit, and take as long as you need to do it.

I know some people have unfixable relationships with their family because of damn good reasons, like abuse or addictions. In that case, I hope people can find a mentor or somebody to take their parents' place. I couldn't imagine how bad it would be if I couldn't go to my parents for love and support. We all need someone to count on, who we can turn to. However you put a family together, those strong ties are your emotional safety net. It's always there for you.

Boyfriends come and go. Friends come and go.

Family is here to stay. That's why it's called family.

CHAPTER SEVEN

Strong Base

've had a long love affair with the Dollar Store. I've been going there since I was a kid, when my crafty side was only just start-ing to emerge. I remember buying $1 terra-cotta pots when I was in elementary school, and painting vines and flowers on them to give as gifts.

As an adult, I still hit up that place. I could wander the aisles for hours, throwing random crap into my basket and then turn it into something useful. For a while, I was obsessed with duct tape. I made wallets and purses out of it for my friends. Some might think of a homemade wallet made from Dollar Store duct tape as cheap crap. I think of it as inexpensive-yet-classy.

One of my life philosophies is, *Why spend $3 when you can spend $1?* When I was on *Dancing with the Stars,* I thought it'd be cute to give my fellow competitors and dancers their very own Snooki Slippers. After hours of dancing in heels, you really needed pillows for your feet. So I asked a member of my team to put the slippers in gift bags for everyone. He went to Walmart or wherever, and came back with a big pile of $3 gift bags. My first thought—and the first thing to come out of my mouth—was, "Why didn't you go to the Dollar Store?"

I can't help it, I just love a bargain. The word *sale* makes me wet my panties. If I can save a few bucks by buying one hundred rolls of toilet paper, I do it (I know it'll get used eventually, especially in my house). I drive a reliable truck, not a sports car that'll break down if I look at it funny. I don't spend a fortune on my clothes. I'm still shopping at the same places I always have. Mandee and Bebe, I can't quit you! Jionni and I don't take extravagant vacations. We haven't been on a honeymoon (yet). When we go away, it's to Atlantic City or Florida. Jionni and I are both way into Disney World. I'd rather go to Myrtle Beach with my dad than drop thousands of dollars to fly to some exotic island. I can mix a pina colada in my kitchen and get sun and sand a half hour from my house.

As soon as I started making money, I told myself, "You are not going to be stupid and blow through it in a year," like so many other celebrities have done before me, and will do after me. So many overnight successes wind up bankrupt, in prison, and in debt because they think their income will last forever. They burn through money like it's on fire. In some corners of the celebrity universe, people feel like they have to throw money around to maintain the image or lifestyle they present on their shows.

I was never in danger of doing that. The lifestyle on my shows was low (no) rent, which is exactly how I was living. No fake bull-shit. Keeping it real is what saved me from losing my soul—and my money—while on TV. I also have my dad to keep my finances in order. He's been advising me about investing and budgeting since the be-ginning. Thanks to him and my natural cheapness, I've accumu-lated a nice rainy day fund. Sure, I indulged my shoe addiction now and again, but I didn't go crazy on anything else. I did ten seasons on MTV, and I managed to hang on to nearly everything I earned.

One way I saved all that money was by living at home. During *Jersey Shore*, my off-season residence was at home with Mom in Marlboro, New York. I liked living there with her, and my cats and dog. During the summers, I lived in the shore house. While filming *Snooki & Jwoww* season one, Jenni and I shared an apartment in Jersey City. After that, I moved into Jionni's parents' basement for the next few years. I know it seems weird to live with your future in-laws for so long, but it's sort of what you do in my world. (It's an Italian thing.)

For the first twenty-seven years of my life, I didn't live alone or on my own, which was fine by me. I saved up, and had good company. If I had lived alone, I might've starved since I had no idea how to cook. Having kids is what pushed me to get a place of my own. Otherwise, I could probably have mooched off relatives forever and show my gratitude by gifting them duct tape lamp shades and duct tape furniture covers.

When Lorenzo arrived, Jionni and I divided our basement lair into "rooms," so it seemed like we each had our own space. Lorenzo has his crib "room." Jionni had the kitchenette and the "living room." I had my "bedroom." But it was really just one big underground room with no windows for three people along with all of our stuff. We were busting out at the seams.

Jionni and I decided it'd be healthier for the three of us to live above ground in a real house with proper air circulation. The decision to build our dream house was the easy part. Designing, constructing, and moving in to said house? That was freakin' hard. First we had to find an empty lot close to Jionni's family in a good neighborhood to raise kids. We liked this one area in North Jersey that was only half developed. The builders were creating subdivisions as they went along. We were lucky to find the vacant lot when we did, and we went for it. We bought the patch of dirt. It was the most I'd ever spent on any one thing in my life (it cost more than $1). The house itself would not be cheap, either. But if we poured our savings into one thing, let it be where we'd spend most of our time and make our memories.

We worked closely with the builder on the design. I said to him, "I want a walk-in closet, a minimum of five bedrooms, a huge master bathroom, and a home gym."

Jionni had his heart set on superhigh ceilings. He was very particular about the first floor. Just off the kitchen, he wanted a great room where we'd hang out most of the time. (Right now, I'm sitting in that room, and the floor is covered with toys and junk. The entire house is like a giant toy box.) Jionni's vision was to have a wide open space, so you could see clear across the entire first floor, from one end of the kitchen where the stove is, to the other side of the house. He said, "I want everything big and open." Maybe he was reacting to living in a basement for so long. Jionni also wanted a bar in the basement with a real pub feel.

That inspired me to add one more thing to my list. "And a wine cellar," I said. "For wine."

The anticipated six-month building time turned into a year and a half. During the construction, I got pregnant with Giovanna. If they didn't hurry up and finish our house, we'd be a family of four in the basement. It was a cramped time. We felt trapped down there under a mountain of crap. I felt claustrophobic in my own body, carrying this new baby. It was double the stress in what felt like half the already small space. Janice's house is beautiful, and we loved living with Jionni's parents. But we had to get the hell out of there before I seriously flipped shit.

To prevent a total meltdown, I fixated on decorating the house. Pinterest was my go-to place for inspiration. I'd spend hours a day searching for DYI home decor ideas. I'd see something that looked good—end tables or a glass candy dish—and go to the wholesale supplies stores for basic materials, gold spray paint, wood, glass, a glue gun, etc. My table would look exactly the same as a fancy storebrand item at one-tenth the price. Arts and crafts isn't only fun, it saves you big bucks.

I picked out everything for the home, every paint color, piece of furniture, bathroom fixture, slab of granite, and square of tile. I didn't hire an interior designer or anything. If I had to give credit where it's due, I'd say we decorated our house by the Dollar Store.

I'm glad I didn't have the money or inclination to build a dream house five years ago. Snooki's Dream House would look a lot different than Nicole's. Snooki's would be covered in leopard-print wallpaper, with a stripper pole and a hot tub in the living room. I am so over animal print and pink. My taste has evolved, as I have, from trashy to classy.

I was eight-months pregnant on our moving day. I felt like Giovanna was going to break through my belly button and rip my stomach open. Ideally, I would have rested with my swollen feet up. But I had to run around buying house supplies and packing for the move. Only a maniac would plan to move, then have a baby, then get married, in the span of three months. I still can't believe we survived.

For non-DIY furniture, I ordered a lot online to be delivered. I got stuff from One Kings Lane and Wayfair, and some designer items on sale. I spent more than I thought I would on furniture, but that's okay. I didn't want to sit on a cheap chair, and break it. Jionni would never let me forget that.

Some of the furniture arrived all set up and ready to go. Other stuff came in a million pieces, a plastic bag full of screws and bolts, and instructions on how to put it together. I tried to put a cabinet together for my powder room, starting the job in the morning with great enthusiasm. The instructions were pretty simple. Put part A into part B and insert screw C into hole D. But when I took a closer look, the photos in the directions didn't seem to match the pieces in the box. I did my best, but I could not figure out how to make it fit. I worked up a sweat with the screwdriver, trying to construct it. My huge pregnant belly kept getting in the way. My back was killing me. I didn't give up, though. I was determined to build this one piece of real furniture, so I could look at it and say, "I made that." It took two frustrating hours to build one damn drawer. Another couple of hours to put up the frame. But, as the sun set, I finished the job. It took all day.

Jionni came in to inspect the job I did. He took one look at the cabinet and said, "Are you serious?" He pointed out a few weird places, some screws that were sticking out randomly, not actually screwed into anything but air.

I said, "I followed the directions."

"It's only a few steps. How could you mess it up?" he asked.

Asshole! I reminded him of the time he thought he could follow the directions to build a backyard swing set for Lorenzo. Ha! We had to call in professionals.

I said, "It's fine," and put a vase on top of the cabinet.

It seemed to shudder for a second, and then collapsed. It completely fell apart. Either the manufacturer sucked, or I did.

A whole day, wasted. But it was almost worth it for how hard we laughed over the pile of parts and screws on the floor.

I almost posted a photo of the pile on Instagram with the caption, "No one said I was good handyman." But I didn't. Everyone already thinks I'm a slut. I wasn't going to give them a "handyman" comment. I knew what the haters would say.

Moving day was exhausting but we got it done. We'd only just finished unpacking the boxes when I went into labor with Giovanna. We left the hospital and brought our baby here, to our home, to her room that was ready for her. (She never sleeps there, FYI. She's with me; I'm breastfeeding.) It was such a different feeling to bring Giovanna to our own home rather than bringing Lorenzo to Jionni's parents' house. I felt like a real person, a real grown-up. Jionni and I were independent now. We'd sink or swim on our own. Coming home to the house we designed and decorated together, with the babies we made together, was the best feeling in the world.

❤ ❤ ❤

My favorite room in the house is, without a doubt, my master bathroom and closet. The bathroom is all black and white. It's got a Jacuzzi in the corner that I haven't used yet, but Lorenzo loves to take baths in it. We have a big shower with a bench so you can sit if you like with jets going everywhere. It's like a spa every time you go in there.

Walk straight through the bathroom into my closet. It's enormous, like a studio apartment in the city. It's got hanging rods along both sides, plus shelves. The center island has drawers and cabinets. On the back wall are custom-made shoe shelves that hold my precious collection of heels—about a hundred pairs—and handbags. Sometimes, I just walk in my closet, and stare at my shoes. To see them all arranged like that, in an open, sunny space, fills my heart with joy. Does that make me shallow? I don't friggin' care. I get emotional about my shoes. If you could see them, you would, too.

Also in the closet, I have a makeup table with professional lighting around a huge mirror. Unless I'm doing a photo shoot (sometimes even then), I do my own hair and makeup for events, appearances, and nights out. In my fabulous new closet, I sit at my makeup table, with all my brushes and tools, bottles and jars, my flat iron and blow-dryer, around me. I can spread out and really see what I'm doing. It's an everyday luxury that I will never take for granted.

My second favorite space in the house is my crafts room in the attic. It's my version of a man cave. The crafts space is my retreat. Making things is relaxing and gives me a feeling of accomplishment. I'm so calm in the attic, I don't mind the spiders up there, which, coming from me, says a lot. After I put the kids to bed, I climb the stairs to my little haven, and stay up all hours of the night making picture frames, mugs, jewelry, dance bags, all kinds of stuff. A piece might start as wholesale junk. By the time I'm finished, it's a masterpiece. Welp, not always. Sometimes my crafts look like a two-year-old made them. But most of my goods are professional enough to sell at my Etsy store called, appropriately, Nicole's Craft Room. I also use the attic as a wrapping room. One of my favorite things to do in life is wrap presents for Christmas. I love to give out presents that make people's eyes get big. I get a little crazy with the ribbons and bows and I make a mess with snippets and empty cardboard tubes. Jionni should be grateful. Wrapping in the attic keeps the rest of the house from being a mess, too. (But it is anyway. Like I said, I live in the biggest toy box in the world.)

The home gym exists, in theory. The room is completely empty right now. One day, we'll buy equipment, but in the meantime, it's just a big empty space, waiting to be filled, like a vagina.

Now that we've settled in, I see what I was missing all those years of living in someone else's house. Having our own place is a total game changer. One of the benefits is that we can walk around naked and not feel weird. I'm pretty sure the very first caveman who branched out into his own cave did it so he could let his balls swing free in the fresh air. Jionni does it all the time. I approve. The man works hard. If he wants to air out his nuts, he should go right ahead. If he wants to invite friends over to watch, he could. If we want to throw parties, or have barbecues, or whatever, dressed or naked, we don't need to ask permission or check anyone's schedule. It's our house. We can do whatever we want.

I can't express enough how important it is to have a place to call your own, to feather it with things that make you feel safe and happy, and to invite friends and family into it. You start a life of your own when you have your own home. (I might embroider that on a pillow, too.)

Now that I have a home, I feel like I can grow into it, really settle in and fill up all the bedrooms with babies. But I also feel like I can grow beyond these walls now that I have this secure home base to come back to. I have my place in the world. The hard part is settled. It's taken care of. Now all the energy I used to put into moving place to place can be devoted to my kids and my crafts, aka my little masterpieces.

CHAPTER EIGHT

Strong Guts

I'm not a "star." I'm a normal person who happened to be on a reality show. So I felt a bit ambivalent about appearing on *Dancing with the Stars* for that reason alone. I was not part of the dance world, either. *What are these dance people going to be like?* I thought they'd be high maintenance and weird. But when I got there, everyone made me feel relaxed and comfortable.

Sasha Farber, my professional dancer partner, and I clicked immediately into a brother-sister relationship. We got real close, real fast. Within five minutes of meeting each other, he'd felt me up all over. When you dance with someone, you get physically closer than Anthony Michael and I ever had. Sasha touched me in more ways and places than my husband. I was completely dependent on Sasha, like a hostage or a coma patient.

I didn't know any of the moves, or how to learn them. He had to teach me every single nuance. Sometimes, that meant grabbing my ass to show me how to shake it. If I had any modesty about my body before the show, working with Sasha made me throw them out the window.

One time, he was teaching me a move and lifted me above his head. He had to look up, right into my crotch. Kewl. When he let me down, he said, "Hey, babe. You need to put your string away."

"My what?"

He just pointed at my crotch. "Your string."

I was wearing shorts and was in such a rush to get to our rehearsal, I forgot to put underwear on. My tampon string was in view. He was so close to it, he could have caught it in his teeth and pulled it out. My husband doesn't even see that. I couldn't hide anything from Sasha, not my string, my lack of dancing skills, my insecurities. He saw everything about me. There were no walls between us. I grew to trust this man like my own family. We're close friends still. He came to my wedding and we text every day. It pisses me off he hasn't been partnered with a "star" since me. He's short and he needs a short partner. I hope they find someone for him.

My best friend, aside from Sasha Farber, on *DWTS* was Leah Remini. I loved her on *The King of Queens*. As soon as I saw her, I went right up to her, and said, "I wanna meet this bitch."

Leah is still that girl from Brooklyn. She's always totally herself. She doesn't give a shit about anything, which I love about her. (And what she likes about me.)

The security guards and all the pros told us our season was the most fun to be a part of because we would round up everyone to get a drink after. Leah's theory is that it's an East Coast thing, to say, "Hey, let's go get a drink." Some nights, Leah, Cheryl Burke, and I would stay out late, pounding shots and laughing our asses off.

Some of the questions I get asked most often about *DWTS* are . . .

WERE YOU NERVOUS?

Hell yeah! On the days of the show's live broadcasts, Leah and I always sat together, freaking out. The best way to make a fast friend? Shit your pants, side by side. Leah thought I was a rock because I kind of shut down when I'm nervous, like an earthquake inside. But she eventually understood that I was literally freaking out all day long. I would run to the bathroom every hour, on the hour, with nervous poops. By the third or fourth week, that calmed down. I always got butterflies during the first minute of the dance, but once you get going, you remember the steps and it all flows. It kind of reminded me of cheerleading competitions, only with just me and Sasha out there.

WHERE DO YOU GET THE COSTUMES?

The costumes were definitely extreme. I know they look insane on TV, but I liked mine. Sasha picked out our costumes perfectly. They didn't show too much skin. Sure, for some of the dancers, the costumes show everything. But mine covered up my stomach. I'd just had Lorenzo; I didn't want to flash my sexy stretch marks and loose skin to an audience of millions.

WHO PICKED THE MUSIC?

The pros do it all. They pick the music, the costumes, and the props. They choreograph the dances. As hard as I worked, Sasha worked ten times harder. I couldn't picture myself doing it with anyone else. I had to be with someone who knows how to have fun and not take it too seriously. There were a couple of dancers in my season that took the whole thing so seriously, it wasn't fun at all. But Sasha and I kept it in perspective. You can work your ass off, and go for great, without driving yourself nuts.

HOW MUCH DO YOU GET PAID?

I'm not going to open up my bank statements. You can Google that kind of info if you're really curious. Generally, you get a certain number to appear on the show at all. Then you get more money for each week you last. There are bonuses, too, if you make it past a certain number of weeks. The winner gets paid *a lot.* I'm not sure how much the pros get paid.

DID YOU MOVE TO L.A. TO DO THE SHOW?

The show tapes in Los Angeles, but I didn't want to leave my family for the run of the show. Lorenzo was a baby, and I was so attached to him and Jionni. Usually, if you're based on the East Coast, the show gives you a place to live until you're voted off. But I insisted on going back to New Jersey during the week. Poor Sasha had to do the same so we could keep practicing. After the live show, I took the red eye from L.A. to NYC. Learning the routines and practicing was double draining for me because of that choice. It took a physical toll, and an emotional one. Each time I had to leave Lorenzo, I was devastated. I cried on the flight out, and then had to get my energy back up to learn the routines and perform them at the highest level I could pull off back in L.A.

DID YOU LOSE WEIGHT?

Everyone was like, "Oh, you lost so much weight on Dancing with the Stars." Not true. I lost *muscle*. I'd been hardcore training with Anthony before I did DWTS and built up muscle. Then I did the show and stopped weight training. Dancing is all cardio, which makes your muscles smaller. I was pissed off.

HERE'S MOM

I was pretty amazed watching Nicole on DWTS. She has a background in gymnastics, but that was ten years ago. Cheerleading takes a lot of coordination and skill, but it's not dancing. I don't think cheerleading and, say, the jitterbug have much in common anyway.

When she was first approached about doing the show, she was skeptical. Could she do it? Once she decided that it was worth trying, she was determined to make it work. Nicole seems to have no fear. She will try anything and just jumps in head first. Honestly, I'm envious of that quality. It's remarkable what you can do if you can push aside fear or figure out a way to take it in stride.

Nicole is terrified of the little things, like spiders. She screams if she sees one. But the idea of dancing in front of millions of people on live TV didn't throw her. There's definitely something in her personality that seeks out and thrives on being in new situations that would be frankly terrifying to most people.

Going on a reality show, for example. Most people would say, "No way." But Nicole wanted to be on one. When she was a teenager, she'd watch reality TV, and said, "I could kill it on a show like that."

I'd say, "Get a grip."

She'd say, "I'm going to be famous one day."

"Great," I said. "In the meantime, go do your homework."

DID IT SUCK TO BE VOTED OFF?

Yes and no.

My last week on *DWTS* was the Halloween show. I'm obsessed with zombies, as my boo boos know all too well. I told Sasha that I had to be one, and he chose the best costume for me: I was a zombie bride with a tattered veil and decaying flesh makeup all over my face, my mouth smeared with fake blood like I'd just been slurping a brain. We did a great routine, and I felt excellent about it.

Then came the announcements of who had the high and low scores. The lowest two scores were me and Sasha, and Bill Engvall and Emma Slater. I didn't think I'd be voted off because Sasha and I killed our dance the week before. So when they said I was going home, my face totally fell. I know it wasn't based on dancing. It was all about votes. Bill had a bigger fan base than me. I lasted seven weeks and danced my balls off. I did my best and left it all on the stage. I have no regrets about my performances. But it would have been cool to last a while longer.

I started crying. So there was my ugly cry face in zombie makeup, made worse by exhaustion and dehydration from shitting nervous diarrhea for the last two months. Sad Zombie: not my best look. Honestly? I was crying partially with relief. I was drained from flying cross-country all that time. I was like, "This sucks, and thank God."

The very next day, I had to do a lot of press for the "I'm a loser" media tour that all voted-off rejects have to make. I told the interviewers that it was bittersweet. I'd cried on national TV, but I finally got to get a pedicure. The dancers weren't allowed to get them during their run to keep their feet callused and tough. I was walking around with Hobbit feet for a couple of months—sexy! So having soft heels and nicely clipped toenails was a joyful relief. The best part about being voted off was going home to Jionni and Lorenzo.

I didn't expect to miss my newly adopted *DWTS* family as much as I did. Unless you were on the show and had your talent, determination, and character tested each week as part of the competition, you can't really understand what it's like. The people who do it become warriors together. Being yanked out of that closeness and intensity made me feel a little lonely, a bit let down.

In the weeks after the show ended for me, I thought a lot about the experience of it. It was intense. I didn't fall on my ass. I felt proud of the work I did. I had a blast with the other contestants and pros (with some notable exceptions). I learned that parts of me are a lot stronger than I realized—like my ankles! If I hadn't rushed into this sequined, glittery world, I wouldn't have made lifelong friends of Sasha and Leah, and learned the difference between a waltz and a cha-cha. The entire *DWTS* experience was something

I look back on with a smile. If I'd been afraid of pushing my limits and testing what I'm capable of, I would have deprived myself of the fun and the memories.

♥ ♥ ♥

Is it stupidity or strength to say, "I might fall on my face, but I'm going for it anyway?" If I hadn't had that attitude, I wouldn't have auditioned for the reality show that changed my life. I never thought I'd be a clothing designer or an author or a music producer, until I threw caution to the wind and went for it.

Leah Remini is a wise woman. On the subject of facing your fears and saying yes even when you don't know what's going to happen, she told me, "There's no rulebook in the business we're in. People had an idea what I should be doing after *King of Queens*. Why do I say no to certain things? Why say yes? I should do things that scare me. If you're not outside your comfort zone, what's the point?"

Shitting your pants is when creativity and brilliance happen.

Sure, it's wise to play to your natural strengths. But until you've tried new things, you don't necessarily know what all of your strengths are. You have to make a real effort to not suck at something before you cross it off your list and say, "That's not for me." *DWTS* critics wrote that I surprised them with my abilities. No one was more surprised than I was that I could pull off a rumba. Not that I'm going pro as a dancer anytime soon. But I wow at weddings.

♥ ♥ ♥

You don't have to shake your bootie on TV to get out of your comfort zone. You don't even have to leave your house.

For me, cooking dinner is an act of bravery.

So I'm living in this house and it has a gorgeous kitchen with Viking appliances. Jionni wanted top of the line because he loves to cook. But it feels wrong to have my husband do all the cooking. I'm a mom and wife. I want to be able to provide a yummy, edible dinner for my family.

Facing my fear of burning my new house to the ground, I decided to learn how to make a decent dinner. I got a healthy cookbook with low-calorie recipes. All of Jionni's dishes are loaded with them. My dinners would balance that out. The first one I tried was honey mustard chicken. I had to make the honey mustard from scratch with balsamic vinegar. It went fairly well. I cooked the chicken too long and it came out rubbery, but edible. Jionni was proud of me, and he ate every bite.

It was a good first effort. Cooking, as I've learned, isn't as hard as I thought. I've been around great cooks my whole life, people who can just throw a meal together without measuring or following a recipe. But when I tried to cook freestyle, it was always a horror show. Now I know that I have to measure the ingredients and follow the recipe exactly. When I do, the food turns out okay. When I made my next dinner—lemon chicken—it was a little too sour, and a little dried out. But again, edible and, on some parts, totally yummy. Each meal is better than the one before. Sometime by the end of next year, I'll be ready for a cooking competition show. Look out *Top Chef.*

There's hope for anyone out there who thinsk she's a disaster in the kitchen. If I can cook a decent meal, anyone can. I made a roast beef last night with baked potatoes and a salad and it totally did not suck. Tomorrow, I'm going to try to make mozzarella-stuffed chicken in a creamy wine sauce (hello, cheat day!) Hopefully I can pull it off. It'll be the hardest recipe I've ever tried, so I'm taking the whole day to make one dish. If I mess up, I'll try it again. Let the kitchen gods be with me!

If I had to say the one thing that drove me the farthest from my comfort zone and forced me to face my biggest fear—the fear of physical pain—it would be giving birth. Pushing a baby out of my vagina is the bravest thing I've ever done, or ever will do.

With Lorenzo, I went into the hospital at one centimeter dilated. They gave me the epidural right away. I never felt full-on contractions, just little pains.

With Giovanna, however, I felt contractions all day long. They were twelve minutes apart, and then ten minutes apart. I told Jionni they were real, but he didn't believe me. He was like, "Just relax, you'll be fine."

I can't blame him for doubting me. For three weeks straight, every night, I'd been saying, "Tonight's the night."

Jionni would just shake his head and tell me, "It's not going to happen." He didn't think I was going to go early. Nobody did. I was doing everything to try and start my labor. I ate hot peppers out of the garden. I rubbed my nipples and galloped around the yard.

One of those things must have worked. The pain was indescribable, like my insides were in a vise. I was rocking back and forth, in agony, while watching Derek Jeter play his last game as a Yankee. We were cheering for him, and I was screaming in pain. Jionni agreed to take me to the hospital. By the time we got there, I was seven centimeters dilated.

The doctor told me that I was moving along fast and would have to start pushing soon. I put the brakes on that train wreck. Even though the epidural would have slowed down my cervix, I had no intention of going through the childbirth without drugs. I said, "Bring it on. Hook me up. Shoot whatever painkiller you've got into my spinal cord, right now." I didn't want to feel it. Pain is disgusting. Why have it if you don't absolutely have to?

Some people really get into their suffering, like it's a privilege to be writhing around on a hospital bed in agony. Fuck that. There's no easy way to push out a baby. If there's something that can make it easier, I'm doing it. If I can avoid pain, I will. Pain sucks the strength out of you. I'd rather save it for when I need it, or when it can do me some good, like at the gym. When I'm doing squats, I feel the burn. That kind of pain is literally making me stronger, so I kind of get into it. But contractions? Forget it. I'll pass.

There is some pain no matter what you do. And there's definitely a bumpy recovery period after. But it's all worth it to hold my baby girl in my arms. Giovanna, holy crap, she's perfect. She came out looking like Lorenzo's twin. It's like having him as a newborn again. Her face has filled out, and she looks more like me, which is good news. You want your girl to look like you, and your boy to look like his father. When I look at both of my kids, I feel weak in the knees from how much I love them. That love also makes me strong as a lion. No matter what, I'll face any fear to keep them safe.

How to Be Brave

What I do to shut down fear:

1. LISTEN TO MY JAM.

Music helps. Both times I gave birth, I listened to Christmas music. Nothing like pushing a baby out of vagina while listening to "Holy Night." Emphasis on "hole." It makes me think of the egg nog, a warm fire and being with family and makes me happy. If I have to get psyched for the gym, I blast my favorite songs. Music always gives me energy and puts me in a good mood.

2. TELL MYSELF, "JUST HAVE FUN WITH IT."

To talk myself into doing anything, I just repeat the word *fun* over and over. It's my mantra. If you're not having fun, what's the point? If you think of whatever you're doing as a good time, it'll feel like a party.

3. SAY IT TO MAKE IT.

On the podcast, I once said it'd be cool to be in a Broadway show. The next day, the media went crazy. People were appalled and horrified, saying, "How dare Snooki think she deserves to be on Broadway?" I'm like, *meh*. I never said I deserved anything. It was a joke, people. Why does everyone take what I say so seriously? I also think it'd be awesome to win the lottery, climb Mt. Everest, or pee 24-carat liquid gold, but I don't expect to do it! The crazy part, though, is that if I give voice to any random idea, it takes on a life of its own. So if making a joke about it actually led someone to offer me a part on Broadway, I'd be open to it. Why not? As Leah said, we should say yes to what pushes us out of our comfort zone. The first step to getting what you want, is saying, "I want [fill in the blank]."

4. FEAR *IS* FUN.

I personally find it fun as hell to be afraid. That's why I love scary movies. You know that moment when you want to jump out of your skin, your heart is racing, and you might barf? That's the best part for me. I scream and then I just start laughing my ass off. When you're scared, all the juices are flowing, including down your leg.

5. FAILURE DOESN'T EXIST.

I never think, "What if I fail?" Failure isn't an option if you win just by going for it and doing everything you can to get it—whatever "it" is—done. Winning the trophy is awesome. But it's also a kind of victory if you really give it your best shot.

6. BRAVE DOESN'T MEAN CRAZY.

Some people do crazy, dangerous things for an adrenaline rush, like jump out of airplanes. That's not my thing. I had a bad experience on a four by four. I was around thirteen, and me and a friend liked to take four by fours down this dirt road. One day, we rode past this cute guy's house, and he was outside watering the flowers in his yard. I turned my head to look at him instead of turning the wheel to avoid a hole in the road, and I crashed. The bike flipped and landed on me. I couldn't breath or feel my legs. I thought I was going to die or be paralyzed for life. I had to stay in the hospital for days with four broken ribs. Not fun. I don't like to go fast on anything since then. So, yeah, I like a good haunted house tour and a *Scream* movie marathon. But climb a rock face or race motorcycles? Nope. I like to test my limits, not my mortality.

CHAPTER NINE

Strong Sex

I lost my virginity at thirteen. Everyone I knew was doing it and I was curious what all the fuss was about. I thought, *If I do it, I'll be cool, too.* But that was not the case.

In hindsight, doing it so young just ... because ... sounds completely insane. If Giovanna decided to have sex in seventh grade to keep up with her friends, I'd be horrified. I can't even think about it. It makes me feel sick.

I've read that girls are now starting at ten, which is, like fifth grade! I didn't even know what my body parts were at that age. I could barely write my own name. Having sex when you are still using training wheels on a bike is just wrong. What's next? Sex in kindergarten? I wouldn't be surprised. Doing it so young does not make you cool. It only makes people think you're a slut. I speak from personal experience. I wish I'd waited until it was the right time for me, instead of copying what my friends were doing.

How it went down: Bernard (not his real name), a friend, and I were hanging out in my house. He was "just a friend," so my parents' didn't worry about my being alone with him. He stole some sambuca from his house and we got wasted on it. The topic of sex came up.

I said, "Everyone else is doing it. Aren't you curious?"

"Yeah," he said.

"So should we do it?"

"Yeah."

"Right now?"

"Yeah."

Bernard was cute, but he wasn't the greatest conversationalist in the world.

"Don't you need a thing?" I asked.

"I've got a thing," he said, cupping his balls.

Oh God. "No, I mean a *thing*."

I didn't know what the word for condom was back then. We didn't have health class in school or learn about birth control. I was aware that having sex is how you got pregnant, and that, to avoid it, you had to put up some kind of force field to keep his sperm from scrambling my eggs into a baby. Bernard did not have a condom in a wrapper in his wallet. He was a kid! I don't think he even had a wallet.

I said, "We need protection."

Bernard got the bright idea to use Saran Wrap. We went into the kitchen to find some. The search for Saran Wrap while drunk on sambuca—trying to do it really quiet so my parents didn't wake up—wasn't the sexiest foreplay I've even had, but we eventually found the box of plastic wrap, and snuck it back to my room.

He took his penis out. Holy shit, it looked nothing like I thought it would. I'd seen penises before on pervs flashing their dicks on the street, and in paintings. I'd caught a glimpse of some of my friends' units. This was my first up-close encounter with a one-eyed snake. It was red, sticking straight up, and had these veins throbbing all over it. It looked like it was mad at me.

I was supposed to put that gruesome monster inside my kitty cat? I might as well shove a banana through a buttonhole.

So Bernard starts to wind the Sarah Wrap around his junk. Watching this made me think of Mom covering up the leftover casserole. Again, *so* not sexy! Finally, when his penis is wrapped snuggly enough to stay fresh in the fridge for two weeks, I took off my underwear and lay down on the bed. He positioned himself in the right place, and tried to get it in there.

It was like attempting to break through a steel door with a twig. There was no way he was getting in. We had no clue what we were doing. The basic mechanics of it were not working, but not for lack of trying. After ten minutes of frustration, we said "fuck it" to fucking. He took off the Saran Wrap and went home.

It could have been worse. A friend of mine used Saran Wrap instead of a condom once. She and her boyfriend had better luck with actual penetration and they had sex. When he finished and pulled out, his dick was naked.

"Where's the Saran Wrap?" he asked.

It got crammed up inside her. Their sexy afterglow was spent digging around in her cooch, pulling out the slimy plastic.

In comparison to her, my disastrous first attempt was bliss.

I eventually figured out how to get it in, and had a string of sexually selfish/clueless boyfriends for the next ten years. It might be surprising to some who think I'm the biggest slut in the tristate area that I've slept with under ten guys (the exact number is kind of fuzzy; I can't remember some of what, and who, I did). I've made out with a lot more. Most of my one-nighters on *Jersey Shore* fell into that category. People think I fucked my way across Seaside Heights and Miami. It's just not true, lovies. I *snogged* my way across.

My first night with Jionni was a blur. I can't remember much of it. We didn't have sex, though. We just fooled around. I'd have had my doubts about him if we'd done more. I was practically passed out. My man is not into necrophilia. I was so sloppy that night, I felt a little embarrassed in the morning. But, then again, I figured I'd never see this guy again. I had no idea he'd be my husband one day. I just thought he was a one-and-done fling.

We eventually had sex, obviously. Jionni has the honor of being the best sex of my life. He's the only man I've ever really felt passionate about. After our friends-with-benefits stage, we fell in love, and that's when our sex life, already hot, went radioactive.

Love is the ingredient that gives sex super power. When you really trust and care about your man, you can ask each other for what you need. You care more about each other's good time than your own. The physical act of touching and kissing and smutting is like saying to each other "I heart you" over and over again. If you said it out loud, you'd sound stupid. But when you do it without words, you can express your feelings without making it awkward for anyone, including yourself.

I adore Jionni and find him sexy and funny. He turns me on like no one's business. He's the stuffing in my calzone.

We hardly get it on at all anymore.

Being a mom has destroyed my sex life.

Let me tell you what your vagina is going to look like after you give birth. It's friggin' disgusting. It looks like a bomb went off down there.

Two days after Lorenzo was born, I made the huge mistake of spreading my legs and looking at what was left of my lady bits. It looked like raw hamburger that had been run over by a garbage truck.

Now, it's totally normal for the vagina to rip when you push a bowling ball–size baby out of it. I expected that, and asked the doctor to give me an extra couple of stitches when he sewed me up so I'd be nice and tight for Jionni later. Welp, seeing all those black stitches make me think of Frankenstein's monster. My vagina had been resurrected from the dead.

I screamed at the sight, and slammed my legs closed. If I could get through the rest of my life like that, I'd never spread them again. Even now, if I close my eyes, I can still picture the horror. That sound you hear? It's me, gagging. I'm scarred for life, seriously.

It took a few weeks before the swelling went down and the stitches dissolved. My kitty healed, but it just wasn't the same. Eventually, it snapped back to normal size, which is a freakin' miracle when you consider that it'd been stretched to Grand Canyon proportions. But sex since then has been painful. It hurts, ladies. Not agony. But it's a lot less fun than it used to be.

People warned me that motherhood would rob me of my sex drive. I didn't believe them, but, of course, they were right. When you give birth, you deliver yourself of a libido. It flows out of your body along with the amniotic fluid and the placenta.

Being a new father wasn't a huge turn-on for Jionni, either. He was exhausted, and not a huge fan of watching me pump my breasts for milk like a human cow. But he is a man, and no matter how tired he was, he found the energy to put the moves on me. I just wasn't interested in it. I would have rather scrubbed the greasy space behind the toilet than have sex at that point. I took pity on him, though, and we had sex when Lorenzo was three months old. I insisted we do it in the dark so Jionni wouldn't see my massacred vagina. That extra stitch might've tightened me up nicely for him. For me, it felt like his braciola was digging a new tunnel.

Forget it. That was the end of sex as I knew it. It's incredible to think that, only a couple of years before, I thought about doing it with Jionni constantly. I had a porno production company in my head, and Jionni and I were the stars. When we became parents, the porno theater in my head shut down. The lights went out. The theater was all locked up. If you pried open the doors, a bat would fly out. Kind of like my vagina.

We managed to have enough sex to get pregnant with Giovanna. After giving birth to her, I wasn't so worried about getting extra stitches for Jionni's sake. Tight? Who cares? The only times we're ever having sex again are to get pregnant with more babies. If I dared to look, I'm sure my vagina resembles a black hole, not that I've taken a look at it recently.

I have no idea what the hell is going on in my underwear and I don't want to find out. I've got my hands full taking care of two babies, making jewelry, and doing everything around the house. A mom's life becomes a long list of chores. Getting stuff done, knocking the items off the list. Sometimes, your heart swells with love to bursting at how blessed you are to get to care for these little creatures. Sometimes, it's kind of boring. And all the time, sex seems like another thing on the list, somewhere between buying diapers and cleaning out the gutters.

Logistically, it's kind of hard to have sex when you're sleeping in different rooms. Jionni's penis is big, but it's not long enough to reach me when I'm sleeping with Giovanna in our room and he's sleeping with Lorenzo in his room. When we do sleep in the same bed, the kids are between us. I have no idea how long this is going to last, with the babies needing us overnight. But we're probably not hooking at night until the kids sleep in their own rooms, and we have our bed to ourselves.

I've heard from older moms that, when the kids get older and you're not as exhausted all the time, your sex drive does come back, and you have a second honeymoon with your husband. Jionni and I didn't have a *first* honeymoon, so I guess we have two of them to look forward to in about fifteen years when Lorenzo is old enough to drive. Then we'll get back to fucking like robo-bunnies. I look forward to that time. But right now? Meh. How is it possible you can love someone to death, and find him sexy and funny, and yawn at the thought of doing it?

My advice to new moms: masturbate.

If you don't already have one, buy yourself a vibrator. Since you don't have time or the inclination to have sex, just power up your

Pocket Rocket or Magic Wand, and take care of business. Lock the bedroom door, get it done, take two minutes to bask in the afterglow, and then get on with folding the laundry.

We have to be super careful now anyway. I feel like, if we have sex, I'm just going to get pregnant again. I am so fertile. My psychic said, "You better use birth control because a baby wants to come out of you." I've been pregnant for two of the last three summers. Not this summer! I've been killing it at the gym and I want to show off my bikini body to drive Jionni crazy with lust that we'll be too tired to do anything about.

In all seriousness, we do get it in once in a blue moon. The urge strikes occasionally. It's so rare, it must be taken advantage of immediately before it disappears. So I attack Jionni when he's least expecting it. We're both so surprised, it's over and done quickly. I feel couples really need to have sex for five minutes once or twice a year. You know, to keep the love alive.

Sex and the Married Girl

Some tips I have figured out and don't use nearly often enough.

1. **Kiss.** I've noticed this among my married friends and in my own life. When you're starting out, you can make out with your man for hours. Kissing is the sexiest, hottest use of your mouth.

But after you've been together for a while, sex begins and ends in the same place. So even if you start out kissing—real kissing—for two minutes, you can tap into the memory of when sex with him used to feel like a raging fire. Personally, I'm not into too much tongue. Guys will jam it down your throat, like they're trying to fuck your face with their tongues. I like kisses to be more romantic, just a slip of the tongue. Be cute with it.

2. **Read porn.** Erotica, whatever. I read one passage from *Fifty Shades of Grey* and had to put the book down to have sex with Jionni. He didn't know what hit him. I think it was the scene when they first did it. I'm not so into dungeon stuff, mainly because I lived in a basement for years, so the whole underground lair sex stuff isn't so new and exciting. I'm also not into pain, at all. It's one thing to read about it, but in real life? No freakin' way. My philosophy of life is to avoid pain, not get off on it. The scene when Christian Grey pulled out Anastasia's tampon and flung it across the room was hilariously disgusting. I'm not sure what's sexy about yanking out a bloody tampon. But I don't judge! Whatever floats your boat. If taking a shit on each other, or taking golden showers, or Tamponplay is your jam, then go for it.

3. **Watch *The Lion King*.** Seriously. It's my favorite movie

in the entire world. That scene when Simba and Nala are frisky and run through the forest with "Can You Feel the Love Tonight" in the background? They tumble down a hill and Simba lands on top of Nala and she gives him the sexy eye and licks his face? Vagina twitch. I swear. Just watch it. You'll see.

4. **Don't count on the old moves.** What used to work might not do the job after you have kids. Jionni and I used to be really into my boobs. But now, if he tries to touch them, I slap his hand way. Breastfeeding Giovanna has pulled my nips down to my knees. They are long enough to poke out your eyeball. I can't stand to look at them, much less have Jionni touch them. No. Go away. Gross.

5. **Role play.** No, I don't mean roll around on the bed and say, "Weee!" One way to make you feel really close to your husband is to pretend the two of you are completely different people. Cleaning lady in hotel and traveling businessman. A teacher and student. We used to do that, but now we're married and old.

6. **Exercise for your kitty cat.** Kegels. Do them. Tighten the muscles like you're trying to stop the flow, hold for

ten seconds, then release. Do twelve reps every day when you're watching TV. It helps with orgasm and to prevent leaks. I should do them more often. When I do jumping jacks, I wet my pants. Thanks, Giovanna, for that little parting gift.

CHAPTER TEN

Strong Beliefs

Wave your weirdo flag high, people! Let the crazy come. If you really believe in something, then don't be afraid to tell the whole world, even if you know the whole world is going to turn around and call you a gullible idiot. Believers can be gullible idiots together. Strength in numbers, fellow freaks!

I'm a sci-fi fanatic. I believe in all of it—aliens, zombies, ghosts. I have a big imagination, or maybe I'm just the type of person who senses, on a deep level, that the Zombie Apocalypse is coming. With all the germs and viruses out there, it seems inevitable. When the bath salts guy in Miami chased a homeless man down on the street and chewed his face off, I couldn't help thinking, *And so it begins . . .*

Admit it. You thought the same thing.

Since I was a little girl, I've seen things out of the corner of my eye. So does Jionni, but only when he drinks. For me, it's the real deal. When we lived in the basement, there was this one time when I went into the dark bathroom, turned the light on . . . and saw a face in the mirror. A face that wasn't mine. I blinked, and the face was gone, but every hair on the back of my neck was standing up.

I get strong gut feelings that someone is watching me—and I don't mean fans at the mall. When I'm alone reading a book, suddenly a shiver goes through my body. It's like a ghost or a demon sat down next to me, or is staring at me from the ceiling. I say out loud to the empty room, "Leave me alone!" Sometimes, I think it's the ghost of my uncle who passed, and that he's just trying to scare me to bust my balls. Not funny! I often have dreams of people who died, including my uncle. The dreams are so vivid. We have catch-up chats, like we're at Starbucks having coffee, just shooting the shit. The dreams are like visits from the beyond, like signs that spirits keep an eye on their Earth families, and still like to check in and say hello.

For this reason and others, I strongly believe there are other worlds out there. I've had a recurring dream that life on Earth is hell, and that when we die, we start our true life. It's Jesus telling me, "Dude, you're in hell, and one day, you're going to see what life is really about."

People who don't have a big imagination and can't open up their minds to the possibilities are limited, I feel. Jionni is like a scientist. If he can't see it or touch it, it doesn't exist. He needs solid proof. I don't need proof. Maybe it's because I'm a gullible person, or that I want to believe. My attitude is, why not consider the possibilities? If people could open their minds, just a crack—especially the scientists—we might learn what's really happening in this world, and other worlds.

Ghosties

I've felt ghosts, and seen them. Maybe I'm a ghost whisperer. But if any of you die and try to haunt me, just be nice, okay? I get really freaked out.

My first ghostie encounter was back in middle school. I would go away to cheerleading camp every summer in upstate New York. We stayed in these old gross cabins in the middle of nowhere. The dining hall used to be a family's home. The family had to leave because it was haunted by an old lady who died there. So they converted the place for a kids' camp? Yeah, not the coolest idea. So one night, we all snuck up to the dining hall with flashlights. When we got there, we saw a light on. We walked up to the window and heard this weird creaking sound. We were all scared but we looked in anyway. I swear to God this happened: A rocking chair was moving back and forth . . . *all by itself.* No one was there. It was just rocking nice and slow, like the old lady ghost was in it. We were all so scared, we ran back down the hill screaming.

Another time in high school, I stayed at my pal Stephanie's weekend house in the country. I went to bed that night, and I felt a presence pressing me down on the mattress. It wasn't pervy at all, just like something was keeping me from moving or getting up. I asked Stephanie about it the next day, and she told me, "Yeah, that happens. My mom had the same thing." They knew the place was haunted and didn't tell me! Thanks for the warning, Steph! I never went back.

Another major contact was when Lorenzo was still a baby. We hired a sitter to watch him for the day so Jionni, Jenni, and Roger and I could go on a double date. It was the first time we left Lorenzo with a sitter for a whole day, and I was on edge. Roger planned the trip. He wouldn't tell us where we were going, and that made me even more nervous. We crossed the border into Pennsylvania, and got off the highway to go to the town of Spring City.

We pulled up at this crumbling, broken-down building that looked like an abandoned school or hospital. As soon as I stepped out of the car, I was overcome by anxiety. I felt like I was going to shit myself and throw up at the same time. I was just flooded with a bad feeling, physically and emotionally, like my bowels and brain were suddenly under the creepy influence of unseen forces.

The sign over the withered front door said "Pennhurst State

School, established 1908." Our tour guides showed up and introduced themselves as members of the Pennhurst Paranormal Association. Mara, a psychic medium, and Jessie, a paranormal investigator, told us about the building. Now it's just a crumbling ruin, but way back when, it was a state school for, as the founders called them, "feeble-minded and epileptic" children. A hundred years ago, handicapped and severely mentally ill kids were basically dumped here by their parents. It was an asylum, like in *American Horror Story*, but just for kids.

Roger said, "Feeble-minded? We should fit right in."

I was so not laughing. Just being on the front steps was winding me up. I was terrified. Jenni, Roger, and Jionni weren't taking it seriously. It was all fun and games to them. The fact that this place once housed helpless, sick kids was sad and scary enough. As we walked through the doors, I thought I'd be surrounded by the ghosties of children. Jessie told us that Pennhurst is spiritually active, meaning hundreds of spirits haunted the place and they weren't shy about talking to and touching visitors. Holy motherfucking shit balls.

Inside, it was dark, and smelled dusty and kind of metallic. While we were walking down the corridor in dim light, someone kicked a ladder that was propped against the wall. I screamed! I almost had a heart attack. That woke up all the spirits for sure. I thought, *I need Jesus. I need prayers. I need Gandhi.* But all I had were Jenni, Jionni, and Roger, who were enjoying how freaked out I was a little too much.

Mara and Jessie had these hand-held gizmos that registered paranormal vibes or sounds. Mara said, "I always feel a heaviness in my chest" when we entered this one part of the asylum, and I felt it, too.

Jessie said, "If there's anyone here, can you make your presence known?"

Roger farted.

Jionni thought that was hilarious. Grown men are really little boys. I can understand a little joke here and there, but they were making fun of the whole thing. That might piss off the spirits, and then we would be in deep shit, in the dark, with angry ghosts.

Mara said, "I was touched three times when I went on a quick walk" through the next room we went into.

Suddenly, something tickled my shoulder.

I screamed and my heart dropped down to my asshole. I thought it was an evil ghosty. I turned around, and it was friggin' Roger. What was wrong with him?

We went deeper into the building. It was completely dark except for our flashlights. I felt a breeze on my neck, like someone blew on it. I turned around, expecting it to be Roger again.

But he was in front of me.

A few seconds later, something touched my back. It felt like a cold wave of pressure. I jumped and my whole body shook like a spider crawled on me. It was not Jionni. I know what his hand feels like. The ghost touch was kind of grabby, like it was trying to make out with me. Scary. As. Shit.

The whole place was crumbling, and I was also afraid the walls would cave in on us. The school had been shut down for decades, and no one had maintained it. Roger noticed in the back of one room, a busted-up tiled bathtub. Apparently, it was used as a water therapy area for the children. Mara told us that she sensed a presence, a severely handicapped thirteen-year-old boy. Jessie put his paranormal device in the tub and said we could try to make an electronic voice phenomenon recording. We had to be very quiet for all the spirits to settle down. And then Mara suggested we talk to the boy.

Jenni said, "Are you scared?"

Roger said, "Do you want your mommy?"

"I'm a mommy," I said. "You can touch me."

We didn't notice anything. To the naked ear, the room was quiet as a tomb. But then Jessie picked up his device and played back the audio, we heard something. Right after Roger said, "Do you want your mommy," a faint voice said, clear as day, "Mommy."

Even Mara, who's heard and seen a lot of crazy stuff, reacted to that, saying, "Holy . . ."

Holy SHIT is right.

Hearing the ghost say "Mommy" made everything worse. It just confirmed that there are ghosties in this world, that they're in pain and lonely, and that they want their mommies. I was overcome with anxiety, and missed Lorenzo so much, it physically hurt. We'd been there for four hours, and I was so ready to go. I got the feeling the ghosts had had enough of us, too. I thought evil spirits were going to start hurling bricks and dirt at us.

It was a long drive home. As soon as we arrived, I ran to check on Lorenzo, sleeping peacefully in his crib. I had to pick him up and hold him.

Another ghostly ripple happened when Lorenzo was around one and a half. The incident was in our basement home. No, I don't mean an incident in his diaper. Jionni and I had to deal with incidents like that two times a day. I was lying in bed with insomnia. It was 3:00 a.m., and I was thinking about what I was going to do the next day, having a conversation with myself in my head, as usual. Suddenly, Lorenzo's toys started going off. The lights flashed, and the music switched on, all of them at once. Ten seconds later, the toys shut off, at the same time. I thought I might be having another one of my dreams, when aliens and demons attack me (I get them most often when I'm pregnant, which is a big reason I thought Giovanna might be an actual demon). I woke up Jionni and screamed that the basement was haunted. He told me that I was crazy, rolled over, and went back to bed.

The very next day, I mentioned what happened to a nonbeliever friend of mine who told me to check the batteries in the toys. If they were old, the toys might go on and off. I checked, and the batteries were *new*. Jionni also said there had to be a logical explanation. "The house isn't haunted by the Woman in Black," he said. Right when he said it, suddenly, a closet door slammed shut. We were totally alone in the basement (where no one can hear you scream). No breeze down there. The only explanation that made sense was that a ghost, maybe a kid who'd been murdered nearby, had come to play with Lorenzo's toys and then, when he knew he was caught, he went to hide in the closet. What else could *possibly* explain it? My in-laws might need to do some ghostbusting down there.

Aliens

No one doubts that the universe is vast and ever expanding. Stephen Hawking said so, therefore, it must be true. There are an infinite number of stars and galaxies out there in countless systems we don't even know about. In all of those billions upon billions of planets, it stands to reason that some of them have an environment that can sustain life of some kind. Earth is not the only civilized planet. For all we know, some planet out there is covered by giant ladybugs.

I'm definitely not alone in believing that aliens have already come here to investigate us. Hello, Roswell? Area 51? Government conspiracies and cover-ups? At any moment, we might be invaded by beings from outer space, or be taken over by alien pods like in *Body Snatchers*. Many Earthlings believe that aliens walk among us . . . right now.

Reader, I am one of those aliens.

Okay, now the truth comes out. I am an alien, originally from Planet Weirdo. My kind tends to be small compared to humans. We have naturally tan skin and are gifted with superlong eyelashes. We have an extremely low tolerance for pain, laugh like donkeys, and enjoy our wine.

Even if I'm not an actual alien, I still feel like one. I can tell that Giovanna is an alien, too. We're going to bond about that in a few years.

I'm so into alien stories, I flew all the way to Texas just to see the hour-long reunion of the cast of *Roswell*, my favorite TV show of all time. It was like dying and going to heaven, seeing the actors together onstage. They told stories about shooting the show and how amazing it was. I was a little bummed that they didn't do a meet-and-greet for us fanatics, but it was still an amazing experience to see the cast in person. I cried three times, almost peed my pants from excitement, and had sweaty palms for hours. During the audience Q&A, I got the microphone and professed my love for them. Then I asked them the question, "Do you believe in aliens?" The audience groaned and the host of the reunion told me to shut up! He was, in that moment, obviously under the control of an evil alien being. I didn't care. It was so cool to be there and talk to them. They could crap on me and I'd still be rabid fan. *Roswell* FOREVER!

Zombies

My second favorite TV show of all time is *The Walking Dead*. I am obsessed with zombies and am ready, even excited, for the Zombie Apocalypse to happen.

On the podcast, I interviewed Matt Mogk, head of the Zombie Research Society (ZRS), and author of *Everything You Ever Wanted to Know About Zombies*. He also appears on the *Walking Dead* aftershow, *Talking Dead,* which I watch religiously. He knows everything from A to Z about the undead, and has been obsessed with skull munchers since he was a little kid, just like me. My first research paper in school was about what do to if a zombie actually showed up at the front door, and tried to eat your brain. The teacher gave me a C with the comment, "This is ridiculous." Bitch.

My first question for Matt was, "If a Zombie Apocalypse actually happened, what would it look like?"

As he described it, first we'd run out of gas. Within a week, no one would drive cars. I knew that's true. After Hurricane Sandy, here in New Jersey, we ran out of gas in two days. Humans would basically be stuck on foot, running from hungry zombies. Not looking good for us.

Next, I asked him about the perfect zombie shelter. I'd wanted to build one in our house, but Jionni rejected that idea.

Matt agreed with Jionni. "If zombies somehow found the door of the shelter, they'd wait for you to come out. Zombies are patient. They'd wait forever. You'd starve in there," he said. So basements, bunkers, and caves? Bad idea. Escaping by boat won't work, either. Zombies can't swim, but if you're stuck out in the middle of the ocean, you'd probably run out of drinking water.

To survive, said Matt, "You need water, food, and shelter. Also, it should be isolated so you're not around large groups of people who will become zombies. So the best idea is an isolated cabin or somewhere in the mountains with a fresh water supply and animals to hunt."

Shout-out to Vermont! At the first sign of zombies, I'm heading up there!

Zombies, to a certain extent, are grounded in science. It makes them different from vampires and other movie monsters. Matt told me a terrifying story of the time he interviewed a virologist who said scientists could create, in a lab, a virus that turned people into flesh-eating maniacs *today*. They could just combine a highly deadly strain of the flu, plus rabies, and suddenly, "an airborne super rabies" could make everyone start foaming at the mouth and eating each other. The virologist said it'd only be possible in the right circumstances, with a ton of money, but it was doable. I had nightmares for weeks after I learned that. Sorry to ruin your sleep, lovies.

Regarding the Miami bath salts guy, Matt said, "He was just high out of his mind" and decided to eat someone's face for lunch. Zombies make more zombies. "That's the real problem," he said. "One zombie isn't inherently dangerous on a global scale. Unless the guy who got his face eaten off sits up in his hospital bed and starts moaning 'brains' and tries to eat his doctors, we're all okay." The Miami guy was a false alarm.

"Just how bad would the Zombie Apocalypse be?" I asked.

According to his research, it'd be a hundred times more bleak and grueling than *Walking Dead*. "It'd be really bad," he said. "After the novelty wore off of watching the outbreak on the news, it'd be a real bummer," he said.

Okay, maybe I don't want the Zombie Apocalypse after all.

Psychics

Are there people out there who can communicate with ghosts?

Absolutely! If there are ghosts, there have to be people who can talk to them.

I brought a psychic on the podcast to talk about what it's like to see dead people. Alex March is my age and super hot. She looks like Megan Fox with tattoos. She's been seeing spirits since she was a little kid. "I started seeing my dead grandmother when I was four years old. I didn't think anything of it. Most kids see psychic phenomena as imaginary friends," she told me. "Adults believe it's not real, and turn it off. As I got older, like in middle school and high school, I'd get energy flashes from spirits passing through me. I thought I was insane," she said.

She finally confessed to her parents why she was such a nervous wreck. "My parents told me that my grandparents were psychic." Including the grandmother that appeared to her. "When I was seventeen, I was put into a coma after I had a severe head injury. I died for a minute. The only recollection I had was of an angel who said, 'Go back. You'll understand this one day.' Not long after that, I did a spontaneous psychic reading that was spot on, and it all became clear."

I asked her if she sees spirits all the time, like in the shower or at Starbucks. "Do dead people come up to you and ask you a favor while you and your partner are getting it on?" I asked. "Do they say, 'Excuse me, I have to talk to you?' in private moments?"

Apparently, life as a psychic is very crowded. Dead people are everywhere. "They're like chalk outlines or silhouettes to me. When I was younger, I'd see them like a real person. Now, they're see-through, like ghosts," she said. "They pop up all the time. I try to tell them to go away, but they don't always listen. They come to me because they know I can see them. I have a green light above my head."

I asked Alex why spirits hang around on Earth. Do they just like to haunt certain people, or are they stuck here? The answer, according to her, is that some spirits enjoy hanging with family members, just to see what's up with them. They try to leave clues, to let you know they're still around, like in dreams (hey, Uncle Ben!). Other spirits, those who died in wars, for example, want their families to know they didn't suffer and are okay before they cross over. Alex said some spirits don't cross over because their death was so tragic, they don't know they're dead. Those are the ones who need to find a psychic to tell them it's okay to go to heaven.

She said, "Some spirits are scared to cross over because they had a heavy religious background. They think they'll go to hell."

Alex tells me that there is no hell. There is no such thing as death. We get sent to a higher level. The spirits call it "heaven," but it's not really a place, but a "higher level of vibration," she described. It's all about vibration. On Earth, the living have vibration levels, too. "Negative people—nasty, ego-driven people who gossip about each other—have a low vibration and are always tired," said Alex. "Positive people in healthy life balance, have a high vibration. Compared to us, spirits are thousands and thousands of times higher than we are. They vibrate so quickly, you can't see it.

Psychics are born with a naturally high vibration, so we can see and hear spirits."

FYI: I totally agree with Alex on the power of being positive. If you are positive and around positive people, you send that out into the universe and it comes back to you. If you are negative and around negative people, you feel awkward and bad. I try to be positive always. Even if I'm in a bad mood, I fake it and feel better instead of just moping around.

Anyway, I told Alex that Jionni thinks, when you die, you go into the ground and that's it. You're gone. "People are fearful of things they don't understand," she said. "If people really think we are just born, live, and die on Earth, they're insane. You can't physically see love, hope, or any other emotion. Psychic mediums feel things that you can't see. Being open makes life more positive, peaceful, and good."

Take that, Jionni!

Alex warned against using Ouija boards or doing séances, because they send out high vibrations that attract the bad spirits. "You're basically saying, whatever the hell can come through, come through. It'll never be something good," she said, creeping me the fuck out. "Séances, are dark. It's not light. You're pulling in darkness."

After talking with Alex, I kind of rethought how much I've wanted to be able to speak to spirits. It's not all tea and cookies.

But after going back and forth with it, she's glad she has the ability. "I always wanted to be a normal person. But then, I realized it's so cool what I do. Why would I want to be normal?"

Amen, sister.

Witchcraft

I love the idea of using the power of nature and emotions to cast spells. Alex also thinks witchcraft is real, and is a believer in the Wiccan religion, but only in the power of magic to heal people. Dark magic? She got nervous just talking about it. "It's evil and should not be messed with," she said. Okay, I won't!

Alex also talked about the dark magic of talking about Karma. "If you wish harm on someone, that comes back to you. When you tell people, 'Karma is going to get you,' that means you're wishing the negative back on them," she explained. So talking about someone's bad Karma brings the bad to your own door. It's a dark magic spell you cast, unknowingly, on yourself. "People come into your life to make you love yourself and to teach you things," she said. "Experiences can't be viewed as negative or positive. In regular situations and everyday life, you have experience just because you need to learn that lesson. Pain makes you a better person. Failure makes you wiser and stronger." Every mistake is a step in the right direction. Good news for screwups.

Vampires, Mermaids, Werewolves

There just has to be something to all these legends. If the legends weren't based on something that actually happened, how could they exist? Someone just came up with the idea of immortal bloodsuckers that have stalked the planet since the dawn of time? Half-human, half-fishes who live in cities under the sea? Half-human, half-dogs that grown fangs and hair during the full moon? These creatures couldn't have been made out of thin air. The grain of truth to the stories gets reinforced every generation because someone, somewhere, had to have seen actual vampires, in actual coffins. I think that the government is totally aware of all this shit, and keeps it from us so we don't all hide in our closets all day long.

You Might Be Thinking is There Anything She Doesn't Believe In?

Okay, one thing does *not* makes sense to me at all. **Time travel.** Pleeze. You'd have be a freakin' idiot to believe in that bullshit.*

---

* Actually, I sort of believe in that, too.

CHAPTER ELEVEN

Strong History

To know where you're going, you have to know where you've been. It's crucial to your future to have a strong sense of personal history.

If only I could remember it.

What I can recall: Five years ago, I was a fat slob at the bar with a fistful of nachos and a pitcher of margaritas. Most days, I rolled out of bed at 4:00 p.m. and was too lazy or hungover to take a shower. I was a wreck. My job was to drink heavily, and fall on my ass on TV.

Last week, I made a round of publicity stops to promote the paperback edition of my pregnancy memoir *Baby Bumps*. I went on one talk show that I hadn't appeared on since the *Jersey Shore* days. The hosts, a man and a woman, went on and on about how different I was. The last time I was there, I guess I might've been drunk and kind of wild. The male host kept saying how much more attractive I was now. (I thought, *Thanks a lot, and fuck you.*) I would have liked to talk more about *Baby Bumps*, but the whole interview was spent discussing how shocked the hosts were that I wasn't, five years later, the same exact person I used to be.

I really don't think it's that crazy. Are those two hosts exactly the same as they were six years ago? A better question might be: Were they the same person at twenty-one and twenty-seven? I bet not.

I've come a long way from the old days. Let the casual observers and talk-show hosts be shocked and say, "How could that person turn into the woman you are now?" My transformation makes a twisted kind of sense. The past creates the future. I wouldn't be who I am now if I hadn't been who I was then.

Jenni and I talk about this a lot. Yeah, believe it or not, we sit down and have serious conversations about life. We both fully acknowledge that if it weren't for our past on *Jersey Shore,* when we slept with vodka bottles and danced with potted plants, we wouldn't have met our husbands, or had our kids. We wouldn't have met each other. Our lives are interwoven. Jenni is like my other wife. So, in a way, I got two spouses out of that show, and I can't imagine divorcing either one.

I used to be the slob on the beach. And now I'm a MILF at the gym. I've evolved, people. I'll probably keep on evolving. In ten or twenty years, I'll look back at who I am now, and be amazed in comparison to be the woman I'll be then. You follow? Complete astonishment at how we change and grow is to be expected. Every day of your life takes you to the next day and so on to a place you couldn't possibly have imagined. I hope it does, or life will be pretry freakin' boring and predictable.

My blurry past brought me the best things about my present. Being a party girl once upon a time made me famous. It launched my business, which is the way I feed my children. I look back at the girl I was with a smile and a groan. She's gone. If I could go back in time, I wouldn't change much about my past—except for a few of my outfits. I wouldn't want to be that person again, though, or try to be like I was. I'm too old for that now. I'm happy to hang out in my house, playing with my babies, not having sex with my husband, and making necklaces in the attic.

Breaking news: I grew up. Back then, I didn't have any responsibilities. Now, I'm a wife and mother, a mortgage holder. Back then, all I had to do was hang out and party. Now, I've got an empire to run. I mean, *damn*, people. My transformation might seem like a miraculous, single event, like a fairy godmother hit me on the head with a wand and I woke up a different person, or like I had a religious epiphany and saw the light or something.

No. It took some time. I was a kid on *Jersey Shore*. When you're that age, you party and have fun. You hook up with random guys. That's what you do. As each year went by, I drank less, and became monogamous with Jionni, had kids, and so on. I got to the stage of life when partying and drinking and hooking up wasn't what I wanted to do. I think you just need to get it out of your system. Go crazy, do shit that, when you look back on it, makes you cringe. Then when you are a mother and married, you don't have any regrets about missing out.

To be honest, I get a little insulted when people say, "If Snooki can change, anyone can change." I wasn't a meth addict. I wasn't killing people. I was just enjoying myself. When I wasn't on *Jersey Shore*, I was home sleeping, trying to work out, being a normal person. People just thought I did that every single night, which really wasn't the case nine months out of the year. But whatever.

I'd never say I reject that part of my past. That'd be like lying to myself. Everything you've done builds to who you are right now. It's all part of the story. It's definitely embarrassing looking at the old episodes. I think, *Who is that girl, and why is she so weird and annoying?* I accept who I was at that time, but I'd rather not watch it. The way I looked, how I talked, the many ways I wasn't taking care of myself—it's upsetting. The truth is, I hated filming. I needed to make it fun somehow so I drank. When you drink, you are a different person. I don't drink anymore. Hence, I'm not that girl.

I can relate to women who say, "The past is the past. It's over and done and there's no point in thinking about it." I agree, you have to think about what comes next more than what happened before. Dwelling is pointless. But I also believe that you can't really focus on the future until you've sorted shit out. That's what Karl Marx (whoever the hell that is; he's either a Communist or the comic with the bushy eyebrows?) meant when he said, "History repeats itself, first as tragedy, second as farce."

Or, in other words, if you fuck up the same way, the first time it's sad, and the second time, it's a joke. You have to learn from your mistakes, and the only way to do that is to think about them, try to figure out what happened, acknowledge a screwup, and then watch out for a do-over. Like when I got arrested and went to jail several years ago. I don't really remember what happened on the beach that day. By the time of my sentencing, I'd seen the footage and thought long and hard about my actions. I embarrassed myself and owed the judge and the people of Seaside Heights an apology for my behavior. I did my community service gladly, and can look back on that whole experience with pride. Yeah, I was messed up, but I put it right, and I will never make a fool of myself in that particular way again. I'm sure I'll make a fool of myself in other ways (don't worry, boo boos!), but they won't result in my spending the night in jail.

HOW BAD TURNS TO GOOD, A TIMELINE

If you take one isolated thing from the past, and you see it as a thread that connects the past and the future, you can understand clearly why it happened, and how it helped you. Even something horrible, in hindsight, can be seen as a crucial step to your future happiness. One awful, painful moment in my past, followed along a thread, made me the happiest woman alive five years later.

August 2009: *While filming Jersey Shore, I was partying at a bar in Seaside Heights when a drunk asshole tried to steal a round of shots I just paid for. I yelled at him, and he punched me in the face.*

December 2009: *The episode with the punch aired on MTV. A public debate about the meaning of it turned "Snooki" into a household name. If not for the ratings boost, the show might've died after one season, but we got renewed.*

August 2010: *During the filming of season two, I hooked up with a little Mario Brother I met at Karma. I called him Bernard because I was too drunk to remember his real name.*

October 2010: *During the off-season, I called Bernard—real name Jionni—and we started spending more and more time together, eventually deciding to be exclusive and falling in love.*

December 2011: *After peeing on six sticks in a hotel room in Las Vegas for confirmation, I learned that I was accidentally pregnant. Jionni and I decided without a moment's hesitation to have the baby.*

February 2012: *Jionni asked me to marry him on Valentine's Day. I was super hormonal from pregnancy, and had a chin-quivering, sobfest of happiness. Soon after, we moved in together, into the basement.*

August 2012: *Lorenzo Domenic LaValle was born. I became a mom, and understood what it meant to love so much, you don't know what do to with yourself.*

September 2014: *Giovanna Marie LaValle was born, and I was twice blessed.*

November 2014: *Jionni and I got married and began living happily ever after.*

So you see? If I hadn't gotten punched in the face, my roomies might not have rallied behind me. When we started to make an emotional connection, the show became more than just fighting and partying, and really took off. If it hadn't been a hit, there might not have been a season two, when I met Jionni. I kept going back down to New Jersey for the show, making it possible for Jionni and me to hang out together. If not for the show taking me out of town to Rome and Miami, Jionni and I might've broken up or gotten married sooner, who knows? Our relationship was drawn out, with breakups and makeups, over the next couple of years. And then we got pregnant with Lorenzo. If I hadn't gotten punched in the face, I wouldn't have my son. I might have some other son, but not Lorenzo. Lorenzo is such a special kid, I know it was our destiny to get his spermie and my eggie together at that time, to create this particular child.

If you have the right outlook, you can trace forward just about anything bad from the past into something good for your present or the future. Try it, and you'll see. What makes us miserable in the present, might be what gives us joy in the future. So don't freak out. Be open to learning, and watching your life unfold. Just saying.

CHAPTER TWELVE

Strong Hunches

Apples or oranges? *Frozen* or *The Lion King*? Pinot or Merlot? Choices, choices. How do we make them with any certainty that we're picking the right one?

I rely on strong hunches, a powerful feeling in my gut, to guide me. Sometimes, the gut feeling speaks actual words to me in my head. The gut voice can be really literal sometimes when it tells me, "You have gas" or "You have period cramps." Other times, it's theoretical, and says, "That thing you're thinking about doing? Don't. It's not right for you" or "That thing? It's awesome! Go for it!"

I've learned to listen to the voice in my gut. Or is it in my head? Who cares? Wherever it comes from, the voice is the boss. The voice knows things. I'd be crazy not to listen to it.

My psychic friends would call it "women's intuition." By the way, it gets stronger after you have kids. I use mine for just about every decision I have to make. Chicken or fish for dinner? I close my eyes and wait for the voice to tell me. Using this method hasn't steered me wrong yet, even in business. I just get the strong feeling to say yes or no to opportunities. Usually I say yes, especially if it's for something fun and demented. When I get the "no" feeling, even if it's for something that seems like a great idea, I go with that first reaction and turn it down. If my gut says "do not go there," I back the fuck up.

I have vision visions, too. Pictures pop into my head. Sometimes, I see shimmering shapes out of the corner of my eye, like the last swish of a woman's dress as she exits a room. But those are just ghosties. And then there are the lightning bolt visions of the future that strike without warning and have been eerily on target.

I'm not really a psychic or a medium. I'm an ordinary person who wishes she were. But, even without the ability to read minds and talk to spirits, I have made some eerily accurate predictions.

When I was still in high school, I told my friends that I was going to be famous one day. When I searched my heart and head for a vision of what my life was going to be like, I saw myself in the spotlight. I couldn't have possibly imagined how that would eventually come about. I don't think anyone, including the *Jersey*

Shore producers, could have foreseen how big the show would be. I recently had SallyAnn Salsano, the creator of *Jersey Shore*, on my podcast and asked her what she remembered about my audition. She said that I sat down and declared that all I wanted in life was to marry a guido and have lots of Italian babies. Another prediction come true!

Even if you can't look into a crystal ball and see a big house and a family to fill it, you *can* visualize your own future. It's all about letting your wildest dreams and desires enter your head. Dream away. See more and more detail about the life you want. And then do everything in your power to match up reality with the vision.

I just knew what I wanted, and what I expected of myself. And then I took the small steps toward that distant goal. I wanted to be famous, so I went to the audition. I wanted to fall madly in love, so I dated my way through a ton of losers until I found a winner. I wanted to be a mom, so then I got pregnant. Even though it was a few years sooner than I thought, we decided to have the baby.

If you know clearly what you want, opportunities will come your way. If you want to be a mother, or a teacher, or a movie star, the first step is seeing yourself as that. The next step is saying yes to opportunities that your gut voice says are worthwhile. After that, a little planning goes a long way.

If you could see my closet, you'd know how much I love to organize. Like my shoes on the shelf, I organize and plan my life, my family's life, and a career that will give my family the best life possible. I also make sure to have a Plan B and a Plan C for the times when the voice in my gut gets it wrong—as it sometimes does (but not too often, knock wood). Shit happens. Plans go screwy. My strategy is to try a lot of different things I love doing—books, clothing, sunglasses, slippers, music label, perfume, bronzer, an Etsy store—and just wait to see which ones are successful. I don't expect each and every venture to be a wild, unstoppable hit. I listen to my women's intiution, do my best, create from the heart, and hope for the best.

When things go right, I'm happy and grateful, but, honestly? I'm not all that surprised. I had the strong hunches, after all. The gut said "go for it." I believe that if I made something I personally love, that other people would love it, too.

Like the podcast. That was a combination of spontaneity and planning. It came about when *Snooki & Jwoww* was winding down. I figured that, after ten seasons of reality, our fans have gotten used to seeing us each week and they'd miss hearing what we were up to. I want to keep that connection going, but to shift the focus away from my family life, and onto just the random stuff I'm interested in. My team and I figured out the best way to do that, decided the solution was a podcast. We hooked up with Podcast

One, and we dove right in and created *Naturally Nicole*. The whole podcast is my rambling about my life and inviting friends on air to shooting the shit. I had no idea it'd take off like it has. But, then again, I had an inkling.

HERE'S JOEY

Sometime last year, Nicole said, "Let's do a podcast." She had a vision of herself hosting a TV talk show, and thought a weekly podcast would hone her skills and help her figure out how to anchor a half hour– or hour-long show each week. I came on for a regular segment called "Spilling the Tea" to talk about celebrity news.

We've been doing Naturally Nicole for about year. When we started out, we didn't get such great numbers. But Nicole wasn't discouraged. She was having her own fun doing the show, and inviting people she liked to chat on it. The show is kind of like recording her phone conversations. If Nicole has a special guest, they just chat for a while. Nicole always gets to the heart of the matter, asking the questions you know are on the minds of fans. Our segments together are no different from sitting around the house, shooting the shit. We make each other laugh and, apparently, the fans like listening to it.

After a few months of doing the show, the numbers

started to go up. And up, and up. Last week, we had five million downloads. It's an unqualified hit and it's always been so fun to do. I just think it's incredible that Nicole says, "Let's do this," and the next thing you know, we're doing it, having fun, and making it work. That's the power of not being afraid to just go for it.

I did not predict that, one day, I'd spend hours a day in the attic and, like a hipster, sell shit on Etsy. Making jewelry and arts and crafts has been my passion and my main hobby during downtimes forever. I kept it to myself for a long time because making mom crafts was the thing I did that had nothing to do with my fame. I make my bracelets and mugs and canvas bags at 2:00 a.m. when I have insomnia. I'm up in the crafts attic of my house hot ironing decals and ribbons on dance bags in the middle of the night, and it gives me a sense of quiet and peace—something every new mom needs. When I started posting photos of my stuff on Instagram, people said they'd be interested in buying it, and I just casually opened up an Etsy store. It's not like the Snooki Store, where I sell my clothing line. Etsy is my mommy business. I just sold three hundred units for Valentine's Day—photo albums, home decor, mugs, and jewelry.

It's a special kind of joy to make and share the things I made with my own hands. Along with the Etsy store, I've been taking my crafts on the road to fairs. The first one I went to, in Leonia, New Jersey, was to raise money for the American Legion Post where the fair was held. I brought a few boxes of my mugs, shot glasses, wine glasses, pen holders, and set up my store on a fold-out table. Because it wasn't a personal appearance, I just wore a beanie and my glasses. I looked, I'm afraid to say, exactly like someone who sells homemade jewelry on Etsy. This one guy drove for three hours from Connecticut to see my table and support the cause. I donated all my proceeds to the Legion, and we did really well. I loved it so much, I booked another craft show in Fair Lawn. I have a hunch it'll be another cool experience.

Some other hunches I have about my life, and the world in general:

I predict that I'll have two more tan babies. One more boy, and another girl.

I predict that aliens will come and save us from ourselves by teaching us how to control climate change.

I predict that I'll have my own TV talk show. And when I do, I'm going to ask George Clooney how often he masturbates, and Rihanna about how to keep her nipple piercing from getting infected. People need answers!

I predict that I will get a boob job in the next five years. After two babies, my tits are like flapjacks. I could play soccer with them, they're hanging so low. The day I stop breastfeeding my last baby, I am going to get my boobs overhauled. I dream of this day. Soon.

I predict that the Zombie Apacalypse will come. But hopefully not before I have all my babies and get my boob job. I'll survive as well as all of my friends and family. We'll live on a mountain top in a log cabin in Vermont.

I predict that I will turn thirty. I even know the exact day this will happen. It's not for a while yet. I've got a few years. But I'm already planning the party.

CHAPTER THIRTEEN

Strong Gratitude

The two most powerful words in the English language? It's a toss up between "I'm sorry" and "thank you." This chapter is about "thank you." The greatest source of my strength, and anyone's strength, is gratitude.

The source of my gratitude comes from God. I've been going to church since I was a little kid. Mom raised me Catholic, and she's a strong believer in showing up every Sunday for Mass. She made Stephanie and me go every week, and pushed us to sing in the choir. My voice isn't so hot. Fortunately, the other singers drown me out. I wasn't into it at first, because I had to get out of bed on Sunday and stand up singing badly in front of all those people. But I'm so glad I did. I'm grateful to my parents for instilling love and belief in God in me. I have that, and it's a quiet strength I tap into every day.

Besides God, I am grateful for the people I love and the experiences I've been fortunate enough to have. My fans have seen a lot of the moments I'm most grateful for on TV, like the birth of my two babies and getting married to my husband. I'm eternally grateful that I have those incredible days on film, recorded for all time, so that I can watch them and remember how deeply felt they were.

After I gave birth to Lorenzo, I had to go into the studio and do those reaction segments on the show. He was just a few days old, and the producers asked me how it felt to be a mom. I was just overcome with gratitude, and started crying on camera, saying that I'd always wanted to be a mom and now I had my baby with the love of my life. The words were so simple, but the gratitude I felt saying them knocked me off my (still fat) ass. All of the difficult emotions leading up to giving birth, and then the drama of labor and delivery, and the relief of knowing Lorenzo was healthy and that we were all okay combined and came out the other side as this one powerful explosion of gratitude. It was intense. It's still intense. Whenever I look at my kids in the quiet moments, or the loud fun ones, I'm hit by it again and again.

Gratitude is the gift that never stops giving.

Being thankful makes you appreciate what you've got, and not feel envious about what you don't.

I want to tell one last story, about shooting our final wrap for the last season of *Snooki & Jwoww*. Jenni and I had been working together and in each other's lives like few friends can possibly be for ten seasons. We'd decided to go out big, filming the births of our daughters and my wedding with Jionni, and then end the series. It was important to both of us to shift the focus away from our families. We could start over with a new show, but *Snooki & Jwoww*, as it was, had to end.

The show wasn't just ending for us. We'd been working with the same producers, camera people, editors, publicists, techies, and crew all this time. We'd have to say good-bye to them, too. That was hard. Who knows? We might work with some of these people again. But it wouldn't be the same.

So Jenni, Roger, Jionni, and I came in for that final wrap, with the guys standing behind Jenni and me seated in chairs. We said how much fun the show had been and how much we loved doing it, and then the last sign-off and good-bye. And then, the joke was that the director would say, "Cut." We'd all get up like it was no big deal, and casually make plans for dinner on Sunday like, "The show is over, but life goes on exactly the same."

While we were pretending to be chill, I was literally having chills. I was sad that it was over. But the main emotion I felt was gratitude to have been on this roller-coaster ride with Jenni and Jionni and all of our fans. It's been the most incredible, weird, wonderful experience. I'm just so thankful that so many people have related to my story and liked me enough to keep watching. Thank you all, for giving a shit about what happens in my crazy life. I'm just so lucky that all of this has happened, and I couldn't be more grateful that you let me into your homes and news feeds.

There's lot of crazy yet to come. Stay tuned, lovies.

XXOO,

Nicole

Acknowledgments

I dedicate this fabulous book to my family—my motivators who made me become this awesome person I am today. To my husband—who makes me want to be a better person every single day. And to my two nuggets—who make me want to be the best, strongest mother for them.

I would like to acknowledge my trainer Anthony Michael for whipping my ass into shape and dealing with my stank ass in the gym. I would also like to thank Jennifer Kasius at Running Press, Scott Miller at Trident Media Group, and my collaborator Valerie Frankel for helping me translate my ideas onto the page.

And of course I want to thank my fans, who have motivated me by allowing me to motivate them! You can always change for the better and become the best, strongest person that you can possibly be. LOVE YOU BITCHES!